An Introduction to Python

Release 2.5

Guido van Rossum
Fred L. Drake, Jr., editor

Python Software Foundation
Email: docs@python.org

A catalogue record for this book is available from the British Library.

First printing, August 2003 (14/4/2003).
Second printing (revised for version 2.5), November 2006 (3/11/2006).

Published by Network Theory Limited.

15 Royal Park
Bristol
BS8 3AL
United Kingdom

Email: info@network-theory.co.uk

ISBN 0-9541617-6-9

Further information about this book is available from
http://www.network-theory.co.uk/python/intro/

This book has an unconditional guarantee. If you are not fully satisfied
with your purchase for any reason, please contact the publisher at the
address above.

Additional section authors:
Using Lists as Stacks and Queues by Ka-Ping Yee
Floating Point Arithmetic—Issues and Limitations by Tim Peters
Unicode Strings by Marc-Andre Lemburg

Summary of changes made for this edition by Network Theory Ltd:

Minor editing of text and examples for layout in book format. Added Publisher's
preface. Moved abstract to introduction. Some paragraphs and sentences edited or
removed for conciseness. A complete set of differences can be found at
http://www.network-theory.co.uk/python/intro/src/

Contents

Publisher's Preface

This manual is part of the official reference documentation for Python, an object-oriented programming language created by Guido van Rossum.

Python is *free software*. The term "free software" refers to your freedom to run, copy, distribute, study, change and improve the software. With Python you have all these freedoms.

You can support free software by becoming an associate member of the Free Software Foundation. The Free Software Foundation is a tax-exempt charity dedicated to promoting the right to use, study, copy, modify, and redistribute computer programs. It also helps to spread awareness of the ethical and political issues of freedom in the use of software. For more information visit the website www.fsf.org.

The development of Python itself is supported by the Python Software Foundation. Companies using Python can invest in the language by becoming sponsoring members of this group. Donations can also be made online through the Python website. Further information is available at http://www.python.org/psf/

Brian Gough
Publisher
November 2006

Introduction

Python is an easy to learn, powerful programming language. It has efficient high-level data structures and a simple but effective approach to object-oriented programming. Python's elegant syntax and dynamic typing, together with its interpreted nature, make it an ideal language for scripting and rapid application development in many areas on most platforms.

The Python interpreter and the extensive standard library are freely available in source or binary form for all major platforms from the Python Web site, `http://www.python.org/`, and may be freely distributed. The same site also contains distributions of and pointers to many free third party Python modules, programs and tools, and additional documentation. The Python interpreter is easily extended with new functions and data types implemented in C or C++ (or other languages callable from C). Python is also suitable as an extension language for customizable applications.

This tutorial introduces the reader informally to the basic concepts and features of the Python language and system. It helps to have a Python interpreter handy for hands-on experience, but all examples are self-contained, so the tutorial can be read off-line as well.

For a description of standard objects and modules, see the *Python Library Reference Manual*. The *Python Language Reference Manual* gives a more formal definition of the language. To write extensions in C or C++, read *Extending and Embedding the Python Interpreter* and the *Python/C API Reference*.

This tutorial does not attempt to be comprehensive and cover every single feature, or even every commonly used feature. Instead, it introduces many of Python's most noteworthy features, and will give you a good idea of the language's flavor and style. After reading it, you will be able to read and write Python modules and programs, and you will be ready to learn more about the various Python library modules described in the *Python Library Reference Manual*.

1 Whetting Your Appetite

If you do much work on computers, eventually you find that there's some task you'd like to automate. For example, you may wish to perform a search-and-replace over a large number of text files, or rename and rearrange a bunch of photo files in a complicated way. Perhaps you'd like to write a small custom database, or a specialized GUI application, or a simple game.

If you're a professional software developer, you may have to work with several C/C++/Java libraries but find the usual write/compile/test/re-compile cycle is too slow. Perhaps you're writing a test suite for such a library and find writing the testing code a tedious task. Or maybe you've written a program that could use an extension language, and you don't want to design and implement a whole new language for your application.

Python is just the language for you.

You could write a UNIX shell script or Windows batch files for some of these tasks, but shell scripts are best at moving around files and changing text data, not well-suited for GUI applications or games. You could write a C/C++/Java program, but it can take a lot of development time to get even a first-draft program. Python is simpler to use, available on Windows, MacOS X, and UNIX operating systems, and will help you get the job done more quickly.

Python is simple to use, but it is a real programming language, offering much more structure and support for large programs than shell scripts or batch files can offer. On the other hand, Python also offers much more error checking than C, and, being a *very-high-level language*, it has high-level data types built in, such as flexible arrays and dictionaries. Because of its more general data types Python is applicable to a much larger problem domain than Awk or even Perl, yet many things are at least as easy in Python as in those languages.

Python allows you to split your program into modules that can be reused in other Python programs. It comes with a large collection of standard modules that you can use as the basis of your programs—or as examples to start learning to program in Python. Some of these modules provide things like file I/O, system calls, sockets, and even interfaces to graphical user interface toolkits like Tk.

Python is an interpreted language, which can save you considerable time during program development because no compilation and linking is necessary. The interpreter can be used interactively, which makes it easy to experiment with features of the language, to write throw-away programs, or to test functions during bottom-up program development. It is also a handy desk calculator.

Python enables programs to be written compactly and readably. Programs written in Python are typically much shorter than equivalent C, C++, or Java programs, for several reasons:

- the high-level data types allow you to express complex operations in a single statement;

- statement grouping is done by indentation instead of beginning and ending brackets;

- no variable or argument declarations are necessary.

Python is *extensible*: if you know how to program in C it is easy to add a new built-in function or module to the interpreter, either to perform critical operations at maximum speed, or to link Python programs to libraries that may only be available in binary form (such as a vendor-specific graphics library). Once you are really hooked, you can link the Python interpreter into an application written in C and use it as an extension or command language for that application.

By the way, the language is named after the BBC show "Monty Python's Flying Circus" and has nothing to do with nasty reptiles. Making references to Monty Python skits in documentation is not only allowed, it is encouraged!

Now that you are all excited about Python, you'll want to examine it in some more detail. Since the best way to learn a language is to use it, the tutorial invites you to play with the Python interpreter as you read.

In the next chapter, the mechanics of using the interpreter are explained. This is rather mundane information, but essential for trying out the examples shown later.

The rest of the tutorial introduces various features of the Python language and system through examples, beginning with simple expressions, statements and data types, through functions and modules, and finally touching upon advanced concepts like exceptions and user-defined classes.

2 Using the Python Interpreter

2.1 Invoking the Interpreter

The Python interpreter is usually installed as '/usr/bin/python' or '/usr/local/bin/python' on those machines where it is available; putting the appropriate directory in your UNIX shell's search path makes it possible to start it by typing the command

```
python
```

to the shell. Since the choice of the directory where the interpreter lives is an installation option, other places are possible; check with your local Python guru or system administrator. (E.g., '/usr/local/python' is a popular alternative location.)

On Windows machines, the Python installation is usually placed in a directory like 'C:\Python25', though you can change this when you're running the installer. To add this directory to your path, you can type the following command into the command prompt in a DOS box:

```
set path=%path%;C:\python25
```

Typing an end-of-file character (Control-D on UNIX, Control-Z on Windows) at the primary prompt causes the interpreter to exit with a zero exit status. If that doesn't work, you can exit the interpreter by typing the following commands: 'import sys; sys.exit()'.

The interpreter's line-editing features usually aren't very sophisticated. On UNIX, whoever installed the interpreter may have enabled support for the GNU readline library, which adds more elaborate interactive editing and history features. Perhaps the quickest check to see whether command-line editing is supported is typing Control-P to the first Python prompt you get. If it beeps, you have command-line editing; see Appendix A for an introduction to the keys. If nothing appears to happen, or if ^P is echoed, command-line editing isn't available; you'll only be able to use backspace to remove characters from the current line.

The interpreter operates somewhat like the UNIX shell: when called with standard input connected to a tty device, it reads and executes commands interactively; when called with a file name argument or with a file as standard input, it reads and executes a *script* from that file.

A second way of starting the interpreter is 'python -c *command* [arg] ...', which executes the statement(s) in *command*, analogous to the shell's -c option. Since Python statements often contain spaces or other characters that are special to the shell, it is best to quote *command* in its entirety with double quotes.

Some Python modules are also useful as scripts. These can be invoked using 'python -m *module* [arg] ...', which executes the source file for *module* as if you had spelled out its full name on the command line.

Note that there is a difference between 'python file' and 'python <file'. In the latter case, input requests from the program, such as calls to input() and raw_input(), are satisfied from *file*. Since this file has already been read until the end by the parser before the program starts executing, the program will encounter end-of-file immediately. In the former case (which is usually what you want) they are satisfied from whatever file or device is connected to standard input of the Python interpreter.

When a script file is used, it is sometimes useful to be able to run the script and enter interactive mode afterwards. This can be done by passing -i before the script. (This does not work if the script is read from standard input, for the same reason as explained in the previous paragraph.)

2.1.1 Argument Passing

When known to the interpreter, the script name and additional arguments thereafter are passed to the script in the variable sys.argv, which is a list of strings. Its length is at least one; when no script and no arguments are given, sys.argv[0] is an empty string. When the script name is given as '-' (meaning standard input), sys.argv[0] is set to '-'. When -c *command* is used, sys.argv[0] is set to '-c'. When -m *module* is used, sys.argv[0] is set to the full name of the located module. Options found after -c *command* or -m *module* are not consumed by the Python interpreter's option processing but left in sys.argv for the command or module to handle.

2.1.2 Interactive Mode

When commands are read from a tty, the interpreter is said to be in *interactive mode*. In this mode it prompts for the next command with the *primary prompt*, usually three greater-than signs ('>>> '); for continuation lines it prompts with the *secondary prompt*, by default three dots ('... ').

The interpreter prints a welcome message stating its version number and a copyright notice before printing the first prompt:

```
python
Python 2.5 (r25:51908, Nov 18 2006, 11:52:11)
Type "help", "copyright", "credits" or "license"
for more information.
>>>
```

Continuation lines are needed when entering a multi-line construct. As an example, take a look at this if statement:

```
>>> the_world_is_flat = 1
>>> if the_world_is_flat:
...     print "Be careful not to fall off!"
...
Be careful not to fall off!
```

2.2 The Interpreter and Its Environment

2.2.1 Error Handling

When an error occurs, the interpreter prints an error message and a stack trace. In interactive mode, it then returns to the primary prompt; when input came from a file, it exits with a nonzero exit status after printing the stack trace. (Exceptions handled by an except clause in a try statement are not errors in this context.) Some errors are unconditionally fatal and cause an exit with a nonzero exit status; this applies to internal inconsistencies and some cases of running out of memory. All error messages are written to the standard error stream; normal output from executed commands is written to standard output.

Typing the interrupt character (usually Control-C or DEL) to the primary or secondary prompt cancels the input and returns to the primary prompt. Typing an interrupt while a command is executing raises the KeyboardInterrupt exception, which may be handled by a try statement.

2.2.2 Executable Python Scripts

On BSD'ish UNIX systems, Python scripts can be made directly executable, like shell scripts, by putting the line

```
#! /usr/bin/env python
```

(assuming that the interpreter is on the user's PATH) at the beginning of the script and giving the file an executable mode. The '#!' must be the first two characters of the file. On some platforms, this first line must end with a UNIX-style line ending ('\n'), not a Mac OS ('\r') or Windows ('\r\n') line ending. Note that the hash, or pound, character, '#', is used to start a comment in Python.

The script can be given an executable mode, or permission, using the chmod command:

```
$ chmod +x myscript.py
```

2.2.3   Source Code Encoding

It is possible to use encodings different than ASCII in Python source files. The best way to do it is to put one more special comment line right after the #! line to define the source file encoding:

```
# -*- coding: encoding -*-
```

With that declaration, all characters in the source file will be treated as having the encoding *encoding*, and it will be possible to directly write Unicode string literals in the selected encoding. The list of possible encodings can be found in the *Python Library Reference Manual*, in the section on codecs.

For example, to write Unicode literals including the Euro currency symbol, the ISO-8859-15 encoding can be used, with the Euro symbol having the ordinal value 164. This script will print the value 8364 (the Unicode codepoint corresponding to the Euro symbol) and then exit:

```
# -*- coding: iso-8859-15 -*-

currency = u"€"   # euro symbol
print ord(currency)
```

If your editor supports saving files as UTF-8 with a UTF-8 *byte order mark* (aka BOM), you can use that instead of an encoding declaration. IDLE supports this capability if Options/General/Default Source Encoding/ UTF-8 is set. Note that this signature is not understood in older Python releases (2.2 and earlier), and also not understood by the operating system for script files with #! lines (only used on UNIX systems).

By using UTF-8 (either through the signature or an encoding declaration), characters of most languages in the world can be used simultaneously in string literals and comments. Using non-ASCII characters in identifiers is not supported. To display all these characters properly, your editor must recognize that the file is UTF-8, and it must use a font that supports all the characters in the file.

2.2.4 The Interactive Startup File

When you use Python interactively, it is frequently handy to have some standard commands executed every time the interpreter is started. You can do this by setting an environment variable named PYTHONSTARTUP to the name of a file containing your start-up commands. This is similar to the '.profile' feature of the UNIX shells.

This file is only read in interactive sessions, not when Python reads commands from a script, and not when '/dev/tty' is given as the explicit source of commands (which otherwise behaves like an interactive session). It is executed in the same namespace where interactive commands are executed, so that objects that it defines or imports can be used without qualification in the interactive session. You can also change the prompts sys.ps1 and sys.ps2 in this file.

If you want to read an additional start-up file from the current directory, you can program this in the global start-up file using code like this:

```
if os.path.isfile('.pythonrc.py'):
    execfile('.pythonrc.py')
```

If you want to use the startup file in a script, you must do this explicitly in the script:

```
import os
filename = os.environ.get('PYTHONSTARTUP')
if filename and os.path.isfile(filename):
    execfile(filename)
```

3 An Informal Introduction to Python

In the following examples, input and output are distinguished by the presence or absence of prompts ('>>> ' and '... '): to repeat the example, you must type everything after the prompt, when the prompt appears; lines that do not begin with a prompt are output from the interpreter. Note that a secondary prompt on a line by itself in an example means you must type a blank line; this is used to end a multi-line command.

Many of the examples in this manual, even those entered at the interactive prompt, include comments. Comments in Python start with the hash character, '#', and extend to the end of the physical line. A comment may appear at the start of a line or following whitespace or code, but not within a string literal. A hash character within a string literal is just a hash character.

Some examples:

```
# this is the first comment
SPAM = 1                    # and this is the second comment
                            # ... and now a third!
STRING = "# This is not a comment."
```

3.1 Using Python as a Calculator

Let's try some simple Python commands. Start the interpreter and wait for the primary prompt, '>>> '. (It shouldn't take long.)

3.1.1 Numbers

The interpreter acts as a simple calculator: you can type an expression at it and it will write the value. Expression syntax is straightforward: the operators +, -, * and / work just like in most other languages (for example, Pascal or C); parentheses can be used for grouping. For example:

```
>>> 2+2
4
>>> # This is a comment
```

```
... 2+2
4
>>> 2+2  # and a comment on the same line as code
4
>>> (50-5*6)/4
5
>>> # Integer division returns the floor:
... 7/3
2
>>> 7/-3
-3
```

The equal sign ('=') is used to assign a value to a variable. Afterwards, no result is displayed before the next interactive prompt:

```
>>> width = 20
>>> height = 5*9
>>> width * height
900
```

A value can be assigned to several variables simultaneously:

```
>>> x = y = z = 0  # Zero x, y and z
>>> x
0
>>> y
0
>>> z
0
```

There is full support for floating point; operators with mixed type operands convert the integer operand to floating point:

```
>>> 3 * 3.75 / 1.5
7.5
>>> 7.0 / 2
3.5
```

Complex numbers are also supported; imaginary numbers are written with a suffix of 'j' or 'J'. Complex numbers with a nonzero real component are written as '(real+imagj)', or can be created with the 'complex(real, imag)' function.

```
>>> 1j * 1J
(-1+0j)
>>> 1j * complex(0,1)
(-1+0j)
>>> 3+1j*3
(3+3j)
>>> (3+1j)*3
(9+3j)
>>> (1+2j)/(1+1j)
(1.5+0.5j)
```

Complex numbers are always represented as two floating point numbers, the real and imaginary part. To extract these parts from a complex number z, use z.real and z.imag.

```
>>> a=1.5+0.5j
>>> a.real
1.5
>>> a.imag
0.5
```

The conversion functions to floating point and integer (float(), int() and long()) don't work for complex numbers—there is no one correct way to convert a complex number to a real number. Use abs(z) to get its magnitude (as a float) or z.real to get its real part.

```
>>> a=3.0+4.0j
>>> float(a)
Traceback (most recent call last):
  File "<stdin>", line 1, in ?
TypeError: can't convert complex to float; use abs(z)
>>> a.real
3.0
>>> a.imag
4.0
>>> abs(a)  # sqrt(a.real**2 + a.imag**2)
5.0
>>>
```

In interactive mode, the last printed expression is assigned to the variable _. This means that when you are using Python as a desk calculator, it is somewhat easier to continue calculations, for example:

```
>>> tax = 12.5 / 100
```

```
>>> price = 100.50
>>> price * tax
12.5625
>>> price + _
113.0625
>>> round(_, 2)
113.06
>>>
```

This variable should be treated as read-only by the user. Don't explicitly assign a value to it—you would create an independent local variable with the same name masking the built-in variable with its magic behavior.

3.1.2 Strings

Besides numbers, Python can also manipulate strings, which can be expressed in several ways. They can be enclosed in single quotes or double quotes:

```
>>> 'spam eggs'
'spam eggs'
>>> 'doesn\'t'
"doesn't"
>>> "doesn't"
"doesn't"
>>> '"Yes," he said.'
'"Yes," he said.'
>>> "\"Yes,\" he said."
'"Yes," he said.'
>>> '"Isn\'t," she said.'
'"Isn\'t," she said.'
```

String literals can span multiple lines in several ways. Continuation lines can be used, with a backslash as the last character on the line indicating that the next line is a logical continuation of the line:

```
hello = "This is a rather long string containing\n\
several lines of text just as you would do in C.\n\
    Note that leading whitespace is\
 significant."

print hello
```

Note that newlines still need to be embedded in the string using \n; the newline following the trailing backslash is discarded. This example would print the following:

```
This is a rather long string containing
several lines of text just as you would do in C.
     Note that leading whitespace is significant.
```

If we make the string literal a "raw" string, however, by preceding it with the prefix r the \n sequences are not converted to newlines, but the backslash at the end of the line, and the newline character in the source, are both included in the string as data. Thus, the example:

```
hello = r"This is a rather long string containing\n\
several lines of text much as you would do in C."

print hello
```

would print:

```
This is a rather long string containing\n\
several lines of text much as you would do in C.
```

Or, strings can be surrounded in a pair of matching triple-quotes: """ or
'''. End of lines do not need to be escaped when using triple-quotes, but they will be included in the string.

```
print """
Usage: thingy [OPTIONS]
     -h                        Display this usage message
     -H hostname               Hostname to connect to
"""
```

produces the following output:

```
Usage: thingy [OPTIONS]
     -h                        Display this usage message
     -H hostname               Hostname to connect to
```

The interpreter prints the result of string operations in the same way as they are typed for input: inside quotes, and with quotes and other funny characters escaped by backslashes, to show the precise value. The string is enclosed in double quotes if the string contains a single quote and no double quotes, else it's enclosed in single quotes. (The print statement, described later, can be used to write strings without quotes or escapes.)

Strings can be concatenated (glued together) with the + operator, and repeated with *:

```
>>> word = 'Help' + 'A'
>>> word
'HelpA'
>>> '<' + word*5 + '>'
'<HelpAHelpAHelpAHelpAHelpA>'
```

Two string literals next to each other are automatically concatenated; the first line above could also have been written 'word = 'Help' 'A''; this only works with two literals, not with arbitrary string expressions:

```
>>> 'str' 'ing'              #  <-  This is ok
'string'
>>> 'str'.strip() + 'ing'   #  <-  This is ok
'string'
>>> 'str'.strip() 'ing'     #  <-  This is invalid
  File "<stdin>", line 1, in ?
    'str'.strip() 'ing'
                  ^
SyntaxError: invalid syntax
```

Strings can be subscripted (indexed); like in C, the first character of a string has subscript (index) 0. There is no separate character type; a character is simply a string of size one. Like in the language Icon, substrings can be specified with the *slice notation*: two indices separated by a colon.

```
>>> word[4]
'A'
>>> word[0:2]
'He'
>>> word[2:4]
'lp'
```

Slice indices have useful defaults; an omitted first index defaults to zero, an omitted second index defaults to the size of the string being sliced.

```
>>> word[:2]    # The first two characters
'He'
```

```
>>> word[2:]      # All but the first two characters
'lpA'
```

Unlike a C string, Python strings cannot be changed. Assigning to an indexed position in the string results in an error:

```
>>> word[0] = 'x'
Traceback (most recent call last):
  File "<stdin>", line 1, in ?
TypeError: object doesn't support item assignment
>>> word[:1] = 'Splat'
Traceback (most recent call last):
  File "<stdin>", line 1, in ?
TypeError: object doesn't support slice assignment
```

However, creating a new string with the combined content is easy and efficient:

```
>>> 'x' + word[1:]
'xelpA'
>>> 'Splat' + word[4]
'SplatA'
```

Here's a useful invariant of slice operations: s[:i] + s[i:] equals s.

```
>>> word[:2] + word[2:]
'HelpA'
>>> word[:3] + word[3:]
'HelpA'
```

Degenerate slice indices are handled gracefully: an index that is too large is replaced by the string size, an upper bound smaller than the lower bound returns an empty string.

```
>>> word[1:100]
'elpA'
>>> word[10:]
''
>>> word[2:1]
''
```

Indices may be negative numbers, to start counting from the right. For example:

```
>>> word[-1]      # The last character
'A'
>>> word[-2]      # The last-but-one character
'p'
>>> word[-2:]     # The last two characters
'pA'
>>> word[:-2]     # All but the last two characters
'Hel'
```

But note that -0 is really the same as 0, so it does not count from the right!

```
>>> word[-0]      # (since -0 equals 0)
'H'
```

Out-of-range negative slice indices are truncated, but don't try this for single-element (non-slice) indices:

```
>>> word[-100:]
'HelpA'
>>> word[-10]     # error
Traceback (most recent call last):
  File "<stdin>", line 1, in ?
IndexError: string index out of range
```

The best way to remember how slices work is to think of the indices as pointing *between* characters, with the left edge of the first character numbered 0. Then the right edge of the last character of a string of n characters has index n, for example:

```
 +---+---+---+---+---+
 | H | e | l | p | A |
 +---+---+---+---+---+
 0   1   2   3   4   5
-5  -4  -3  -2  -1
```

The first row of numbers gives the position of the indices 0...5 in the string; the second row gives the corresponding negative indices. The slice from i to j consists of all characters between the edges labeled i and j, respectively.

For non-negative indices, the length of a slice is the difference of the indices, if both are within bounds. For example, the length of word[1:3] is 2.

The built-in function `len()` returns the length of a string:

```
>>> s = 'supercalifragilisticexpialidocious'
>>> len(s)
34
```

3.1.3   Unicode Strings

Python supports characters in different languages using the Unicode standard. Unicode data can be stored and manipulated in the same way as strings.

For example, creating Unicode strings in Python is as simple as creating normal strings:

```
>>> u'Hello World !'
u'Hello World !'
```

The small 'u' in front of the quote indicates that a Unicode string is supposed to be created. If you want to include special characters in the string, you can do so by using the Python *Unicode-Escape* encoding. The following example shows how:

```
>>> u'Hello\u0020World !'
u'Hello World !'
```

The escape sequence \u0020 inserts the Unicode character with the ordinal value 0x0020 (the space character) at the given position.

Other characters are interpreted by using their respective ordinal values directly as Unicode ordinals. If you have literal strings in the standard Latin-1 encoding that is used in many Western countries, you will find it convenient that the lower 256 characters of Unicode are the same as the 256 characters of Latin-1.

For experts, there is also a raw mode just like the one for normal strings. You have to prefix the opening quote with 'ur' to have Python use the *Raw-Unicode-Escape* encoding. It will only apply the above \uXXXX conversion if there is an uneven number of backslashes in front of the small 'u'.

```
>>> ur'Hello\u0020World !'
u'Hello World !'
>>> ur'Hello\\u0020World !'
u'Hello\\\\u0020World !'
```

The raw mode is most useful when you have to enter lots of backslashes, as can be necessary in regular expressions.

Apart from these standard encodings, Python provides a whole set of other ways of creating Unicode strings on the basis of a known encoding. The built-in function unicode() provides access to all registered Unicode codecs (COders and DECoders). Some of the more well known encodings which these codecs can convert are *Latin-1*, *ASCII*, *UTF-8*, and *UTF-16*. The latter two are variable-length encodings that store each Unicode character in one or more bytes. The default encoding is normally set to ASCII, which passes through characters in the range 0 to 127 and rejects any other characters with an error. When a Unicode string is printed, written to a file, or converted with str(), conversion takes place using this default encoding.

```
>>> u"abc"
u'abc'
>>> str(u"abc")
'abc'
>>> u"äöü"
u'\xe4\xf6\xfc'
>>> str(u"äöü")
Traceback (most recent call last):
  File "<stdin>", line 1, in ?
UnicodeEncodeError: 'ascii' codec can't encode characters
  in position 0-2: ordinal not in range(128)
```

To convert a Unicode string into an 8-bit string using a specific encoding, Unicode objects provide an encode() method that takes one argument, the name of the encoding. Lowercase names for encodings are preferred.

```
>>> u"äöü".encode('utf-8')
'\xc3\xa4\xc3\xb6\xc3\xbc'
```

If you have data in a specific encoding and want to produce a corresponding Unicode string from it, you can use the unicode() function with the encoding name as the second argument.

```
>>> unicode('\xc3\xa4\xc3\xb6\xc3\xbc', 'utf-8')
u'\xe4\xf6\xfc'
```

3.1.4 Lists

Python knows a number of *compound* data types, used to group together other values. The most versatile is the *list*, which can be written as a list of comma-separated values (items) between square brackets. List items need not all have the same type.

```
>>> a = ['spam', 'eggs', 100, 1234]
>>> a
['spam', 'eggs', 100, 1234]
```

Like string indices, list indices start at 0, and lists can be sliced, concatenated and so on:

```
>>> a[0]
'spam'
>>> a[3]
1234
>>> a[-2]
100
>>> a[1:-1]
['eggs', 100]
>>> a[:2] + ['bacon', 2*2]
['spam', 'eggs', 'bacon', 4]
>>> 3*a[:3] + ['Boo!']
['spam', 'eggs', 100, 'spam', 'eggs', 100, 'spam',
 'eggs', 100, 'Boo!']
```

Unlike strings, which are *immutable*, it is possible to change individual elements of a list:

```
>>> a
['spam', 'eggs', 100, 1234]
>>> a[2] = a[2] + 23
>>> a
['spam', 'eggs', 123, 1234]
```

Assignment to slices is also possible, and this can even change the size of the list or clear it entirely:

```
>>> # Replace some items:
... a[0:2] = [1, 12]
>>> a
```

```
[1, 12, 123, 1234]
>>> # Remove some:
... a[0:2] = []
>>> a
[123, 1234]
>>> # Insert some:
... a[1:1] = ['foo', 'xyzzy']
>>> a
[123, 'foo', 'xyzzy', 1234]
>>> # Insert (a copy of) itself at the beginning
>>> a[:0] = a
>>> a
[123, 'foo', 'xyzzy', 1234, 123, 'foo', 'xyzzy', 1234]
>>> # Clear the list: replace all items with an empty list
>>> a[:] = []
>>> a
[]
```

The built-in function len() also applies to lists:

```
>>> len(a)
8
```

It is possible to nest lists (create lists containing other lists), for example:

```
>>> q = [2, 3]
>>> p = [1, q, 4]
>>> len(p)
3
>>> p[1]
[2, 3]
>>> p[1][0]
2
>>> p[1].append('xtra')    # See section 5.1
>>> p
[1, [2, 3, 'xtra'], 4]
>>> q
[2, 3, 'xtra']
```

Note that in the last example, p[1] and q really refer to the same object!
We'll come back to *object semantics* later.

3.2   First Steps Towards Programming

Of course, we can use Python for more complicated tasks than adding two and two together. For instance, we can write an initial sub-sequence of the *Fibonacci* series as follows:

```
>>> # Fibonacci series:
... # the sum of two elements defines the next
... a, b = 0, 1
>>> while b < 10:
...         print b
...         a, b = b, a+b
...
1
1
2
3
5
8
```

This example introduces several new features.

- The first line contains a *multiple assignment*: the variables a and b simultaneously get the new values 0 and 1. On the last line this is used again, demonstrating that the expressions on the right-hand side are all evaluated first before any of the assignments take place. The right-hand side expressions are evaluated from the left to the right.

- The while loop executes as long as the condition (here: b < 10) remains true. In Python, like in C, any non-zero integer value is true; zero is false. The condition may also be a string or list value, in fact any sequence; anything with a non-zero length is true, empty sequences are false. The test used in the example is a simple comparison. The standard comparison operators are written the same as in C: < (less than), > (greater than), == (equal to), <= (less than or equal to), >= (greater than or equal to) and != (not equal to).

- The *body* of the loop is *indented*: indentation is Python's way of grouping statements. Python does not (yet!) provide an intelligent input line editing facility, so you have to type a tab or space(s) for each indented line. In practice you will prepare more complicated input for Python with a text editor; most text editors have an auto-indent facility. When a compound statement is entered interactively, it must be followed by a blank line to indicate completion (since the parser cannot guess when you have typed the last line). Note that each line within a basic block must be indented by the same amount.

- The print statement writes the value of the expression(s) it is given. It differs from just writing the expression you want to write (as we did earlier in the calculator examples) in the way it handles multiple expressions and strings. Strings are printed without quotes, and a space is inserted between items, so you can format things nicely, like this:

```
>>> i = 256*256
>>> print 'The value of i is', i
The value of i is 65536
```

A trailing comma avoids the newline after the output:

```
>>> a, b = 0, 1
>>> while b < 1000:
...     print b,
...     a, b = b, a+b
...
1 1 2 3 5 8 13 21 34 55 89 144 233 377 610 987
```

Note that the interpreter inserts a newline before it prints the next prompt if the last line was not completed.

4 More Control Flow Tools

Besides the while statement just introduced, Python knows the usual control flow statements found in other languages, with some twists.

4.1 if Statements

Perhaps the most well-known statement type is the if statement. For example:

```
>>> x = int(raw_input("Please enter an integer: "))
>>> if x < 0:
...         x = 0
...         print 'Negative changed to zero'
... elif x == 0:
...         print 'Zero'
... elif x == 1:
...         print 'Single'
... else:
...         print 'More'
...
```

There can be zero or more elif parts, and the else part is optional. The keyword 'elif' is short for 'else if', and is useful to avoid excessive indentation. An if ... elif ... elif ... sequence is a substitute for the switch or case statements found in other languages.

4.2 for Statements

The for statement in Python differs a bit from what you may be used to in C or Pascal. Rather than always iterating over an arithmetic progression of numbers (like in Pascal), or giving the user the ability to define both the iteration step and halting condition (as C), Python's for statement iterates over the items of any sequence (a list or a string), in the order that they appear in the sequence. For example (no pun intended):

```
>>> # Measure some strings:
... a = ['egg', 'chips', 'spam']
```

```
>>> for x in a:
...     print x, len(x)
...
egg 3
chips 5
spam 4
```

It is not safe to modify the sequence being iterated over in the loop (this can only happen for mutable sequence types, such as lists). If you need to modify the list you are iterating over (for example, to duplicate selected items) you must iterate over a copy. The slice notation makes this particularly convenient:

```
>>> for x in a[:]: # make a slice copy of the entire list
...     if len(x) == 4: a.insert(0, x)
...
>>> a
['spam', 'egg', 'chips', 'spam']
```

4.3   The range() Function

If you do need to iterate over a sequence of numbers, the built-in function range() comes in handy. It generates lists containing arithmetic progressions:

```
>>> range(10)
[0, 1, 2, 3, 4, 5, 6, 7, 8, 9]
```

The given end point is never part of the generated list; range(10) generates a list of 10 values, the legal indices for items of a sequence of length 10. It is possible to let the range start at another number, or to specify a different increment (even negative; sometimes this is called the 'step'):

```
>>> range(5, 10)
[5, 6, 7, 8, 9]
>>> range(0, 10, 3)
[0, 3, 6, 9]
>>> range(-10, -100, -30)
[-10, -40, -70]
```

To iterate over the indices of a sequence, combine range() and len() as follows:

```
>>> a = ['Mary', 'had', 'a', 'little', 'lamb']
>>> for i in range(len(a)):
...     print i, a[i]
...
0 Mary
1 had
2 a
3 little
4 lamb
```

4.4   break and continue Statements, and else Clauses on Loops

The break statement, like in C, breaks out of the smallest enclosing for or while loop.

The continue statement, also borrowed from C, continues with the next iteration of the loop.

Loop statements may have an else clause; it is executed when the loop terminates through exhaustion of the list (with for) or when the condition becomes false (with while), but not when the loop is terminated by a break statement. This is exemplified by the following loop, which searches for prime numbers:

```
>>> for n in range(2, 10):
...     for x in range(2, n):
...         if n % x == 0:
...             print n, 'equals', x, '*', n/x
...             break
...     else:
...         # loop fell through without finding a factor
...         print n, 'is a prime number'
...
2 is a prime number
3 is a prime number
4 equals 2 * 2
5 is a prime number
6 equals 2 * 3
7 is a prime number
8 equals 2 * 4
9 equals 3 * 3
```

4.5   pass Statements

The pass statement does nothing. It can be used when a statement is required syntactically but the program requires no action. For example:

```
>>> while True:
...         pass # Busy-wait for keyboard interrupt
...
```

4.6   Defining Functions

We can create a function that writes the Fibonacci series to an arbitrary boundary:

```
>>> def fib(n):      # write Fibonacci series up to n
...         """Print a Fibonacci series up to n."""
...         a, b = 0, 1
...         while b < n:
...             print b,
...             a, b = b, a+b
...
>>> # Now call the function we just defined:
... fib(2000)
1 1 2 3 5 8 13 21 34 55 89 144 233 377 610 987 1597
```

The keyword def introduces a function *definition*. It must be followed by the function name and the parenthesized list of formal parameters. The statements that form the body of the function start at the next line, and must be indented. The first statement of the function body can optionally be a string literal; this string literal is the function's documentation string, or *docstring*.

There are tools which use docstrings to automatically produce online or printed documentation, or to let the user interactively browse through code; it's good practice to include docstrings in code that you write, so try to make a habit of it.

The *execution* of a function introduces a new symbol table used for the local variables of the function. More precisely, all variable assignments in a function store the value in the local symbol table; whereas variable references first look in the local symbol table, then in the global symbol table, and then in the table of built-in names. Thus, global variables cannot be directly assigned a value within a function (unless named in a global statement), although they may be referenced.

The actual parameters (arguments) to a function call are introduced in the local symbol table of the called function when it is called; thus, arguments are passed using *call by value* (where the *value* is always an object *reference*, not the value of the object).[1] When a function calls another function, a new local symbol table is created for that call.

A function definition introduces the function name in the current symbol table. The value of the function name has a type that is recognized by the interpreter as a user-defined function. This value can be assigned to another name which can then also be used as a function. This serves as a general renaming mechanism:

```
>>> fib
<function fib at 10042ed0>
>>> f = fib
>>> f(100)
1 1 2 3 5 8 13 21 34 55 89
```

You might object that fib is not a function but a procedure. In Python, like in C, procedures are just functions that don't return a value. In fact, technically speaking, procedures do return a value, albeit a rather boring one. This value is called None (it's a built-in name). Writing the value None is normally suppressed by the interpreter if it would be the only value written. You can see it if you really want to:

```
>>> print fib(0)
None
```

It is simple to write a function that returns a list of the numbers of the Fibonacci series, instead of printing it:

```
>>> def fib2(n): # return Fibonacci series up to n
...     """Return a list of the Fibonacci series to n."""
...     result = []
...     a, b = 0, 1
...     while b < n:
...         result.append(b)      # see below
...         a, b = b, a+b
...     return result
...
>>> f100 = fib2(100)      # call it
```

---

[1] Actually, *call by object reference* would be a better description, since if a mutable object is passed, the caller will see any changes the callee makes to it (items inserted into a list).

```
>>> f100                    # write the result
[1, 1, 2, 3, 5, 8, 13, 21, 34, 55, 89]
```

This example, as usual, demonstrates some new Python features:

- The return statement returns with a value from a function. return without an expression argument returns None. Falling off the end of a procedure also returns None.

- The statement result.append(b) calls a *method* of the list object result. A method is a function that 'belongs' to an object and is named obj.methodname, where obj is some object (this may be an expression), and methodname is the name of a method that is defined by the object's type. Different types define different methods. Methods of different types may have the same name without causing ambiguity. (It is possible to define your own object types and methods, using *classes*, as discussed later in this tutorial.) The method append() shown in the example is defined for list objects; it adds a new element at the end of the list. In this example it is equivalent to 'result = result + [b]', but more efficient.

4.7 More on Defining Functions

It is also possible to define functions with a variable number of arguments. There are three forms, which can be combined.

4.7.1 Default Argument Values

The most useful form is to specify a default value for one or more arguments. This creates a function that can be called with fewer arguments than it is defined to allow. For example:

```
def ask_ok(prompt, retries=4, complaint='Yes or no!'):
    while True:
        ok = raw_input(prompt)
        if ok in ('y', 'ye', 'yes'): return True
        if ok in ('n', 'no', 'nop', 'nope'): return False
        retries = retries - 1
        if retries < 0: raise IOError, 'refusenik user'
        print complaint
```

This function can be called either like this: ask_ok('Do you really want to quit?') or like this: ask_ok('Delete file?', 2).

This example also introduces the in keyword. This tests whether or not a sequence contains a certain value.

The default values are evaluated at the point of function definition in the *defining* scope, so that

```
i = 5

def f(arg=i):
    print arg

i = 6
f()
```

will print 5.

Important warning: The default value is evaluated only once. This makes a difference when the default is a mutable object such as a list, dictionary, or instances of most classes. For example, the following function accumulates the arguments passed to it on subsequent calls:

```
def f(a, L=[]):
    L.append(a)
    return L

print f(1)
print f(2)
print f(3)
```

This will print

```
[1]
[1, 2]
[1, 2, 3]
```

If you don't want the default to be shared between subsequent calls, you can write the function like this instead:

```
def f(a, L=None):
    if L is None:
        L = []
    L.append(a)
    return L
```

4.7.2 Keyword Arguments

Functions can also be called using keyword arguments of the form '*keyword = value*'. For instance, the following function:

```
def parrot(voltage, state='a stiff', action='voom',
          type='Norwegian Blue'):
    print "-- This parrot wouldn't", action,
    print "if you put", voltage, "volts through it."
    print "-- Lovely plumage, the", type
    print "-- It's", state, "!"
```

could be called in any of the following ways:

```
parrot(1000)
parrot(action = 'VOOOOOM', voltage = 1000000)
parrot('a thousand', state = 'pushing up the daisies')
parrot('a million', 'bereft of life', 'jump')
```

but the following calls would all be invalid:

```
parrot()                     # required argument missing

parrot(voltage=5.0, 'dead')  # non-keyword argument
                             # following keyword

parrot(110, voltage=220)     # duplicate value for
                             # argument

parrot(actor='John Cleese')  # unknown keyword
```

In general, an argument list must have any positional arguments followed by any keyword arguments, where the keywords must be chosen from the formal parameter names. It's not important whether a formal parameter has a default value or not. No argument may receive a value more than once—formal parameter names corresponding to positional arguments cannot be used as keywords in the same calls. Here's an example that fails due to this restriction:

```
>>> def function(a):
...     pass
...
>>> function(0, a=0)
```

```
Traceback (most recent call last):
  File "<stdin>", line 1, in ?
TypeError: function() got multiple values for
  keyword argument 'a'
```

When a final formal parameter of the form **name is present, it receives
a dictionary containing all keyword arguments except for those corresponding to a formal parameter. This may be combined with a formal
parameter of the form *name (described in the next subsection) which
receives a tuple containing the positional arguments beyond the formal
parameter list. (*name must occur before **name.) For example, if we
define a function like this:

```
def cheeseshop(kind, *arguments, **keywords):
    print "-- Do you have any", kind, '?'
    print "-- I'm sorry, we're all out of", kind
    for arg in arguments: print arg
    print '-'*40
    keys = keywords.keys()
    keys.sort()
    for kw in keys: print kw, ':', keywords[kw]
```

It could be called like this:

```
cheeseshop('Limburger', "It's very runny, sir.",
           "It's really very, VERY runny, sir.",
           client='John Cleese',
           shopkeeper='Michael Palin',
           sketch='Cheese Shop Sketch')
```

and of course it would print:

```
-- Do you have any Limburger ?
-- I'm sorry, we're all out of Limburger
It's very runny, sir.
It's really very, VERY runny, sir.
----------------------------------------
client : John Cleese
shopkeeper : Michael Palin
sketch : Cheese Shop Sketch
```

Note that the sort() method of the list of keyword argument names is
called before printing the contents of the keywords dictionary; if this is
not done, the order in which the arguments are printed is undefined.

4.7.3   Arbitrary Argument Lists

Finally, the least frequently used option is to specify that a function can
be called with an arbitrary number of arguments. These arguments will
be wrapped up in a tuple. Before the variable number of arguments, zero
or more normal arguments may occur.

```
def fprintf(file, format, *args):
    file.write(format % args)
```

4.7.4   Unpacking Argument Lists

The reverse situation occurs when the arguments are already in a list
or tuple but need to be unpacked for a function call requiring separate
positional arguments. For instance, the built-in range() function expects
separate *start* and *stop* arguments. If they are not available separately,
write the function call with the *-operator to unpack the arguments out
of a list or tuple:

```
>>> range(3, 6)    # normal call with separate arguments
[3, 4, 5]
>>> args = [3, 6]
>>> range(*args)   # call with arguments unpacked from list
[3, 4, 5]
```

In the same fashion, dictionaries can deliver keyword arguments with the
**-operator:

```
>>> def parrot(voltage, state='a stiff', action='voom'):
...     print "-- This parrot wouldn't", action,
...     print "if you put", voltage, "volts through it.",
...     print "E's", state, "!"
...
>>> d = {"voltage": "four million",
         "state": "bleedin' demised",
         "action": "VOOM"}
>>> parrot(**d)
-- This parrot wouldn't VOOM if you put four million
  volts through it. E's bleedin' demised !
```

4.7.5   Lambda Forms

By popular demand, a few features commonly found in functional programming languages like Lisp have been added to Python. With the

lambda keyword, small anonymous functions can be created. Here's a function that returns the sum of its two arguments: 'lambda a, b: a+b'. Lambda forms can be used wherever function objects are required. They are syntactically restricted to a single expression. Semantically, they are just syntactic sugar for a normal function definition. Like nested function definitions, lambda forms can reference variables from the containing scope:

```
>>> def make_incrementor(n):
...     return lambda x: x + n
...
>>> f = make_incrementor(42)
>>> f(0)
42
>>> f(1)
43
```

4.7.6 Documentation Strings

There are some common conventions for the content and formatting of documentation strings.

The first line should always be a short, concise summary of the object's purpose. For brevity, it should not explicitly state the object's name or type, since these are available by other means (except if the name happens to be a verb describing a function's operation). This line should begin with a capital letter and end with a period.

If there are more lines in the documentation string, the second line should be blank, visually separating the summary from the rest of the description. The following lines should be one or more paragraphs describing the object's calling conventions, its side effects, etc.

The Python parser does not strip indentation from multi-line string literals in Python, so tools that process documentation have to strip indentation if desired. This is done using the following convention. The first non-blank line *after* the first line of the string determines the amount of indentation for the entire documentation string. (We can't use the first line since it is generally adjacent to the string's opening quotes so its indentation is not apparent in the string literal.) Whitespace "equivalent" to this indentation is then stripped from the start of all lines of the string. Lines that are indented less should not occur, but if they occur all their leading whitespace should be stripped. Equivalence of whitespace should be tested after expansion of tabs (to 8 spaces, normally). Here is an example of a multi-line docstring:

```
>>> def my_function():
...     """Do nothing, but document it.
...
...     No, really, it doesn't do anything.
...     """
...     pass
...
>>> print my_function.__doc__
Do nothing, but document it.

    No, really, it doesn't do anything.
```

5 Data Structures

This chapter describes some things you've learned about already in more detail, and adds some new things as well.

5.1 More on Lists

The list data type has some more methods. Here are all of the methods of list objects:

append(x)
>   Add an item to the end of the list; equivalent to a[len(a):] = [x].

extend(L)
>   Extend the list by appending all the items in the given list; equivalent to a[len(a):] = L.

insert(i, x)
>   Insert an item at a given position. The first argument is the index of the element before which to insert, so a.insert(0, x) inserts at the front of the list, and a.insert(len(a), x) is equivalent to a.append(x).

remove(x)
>   Remove the first item from the list whose value is x. It is an error if there is no such item.

pop($[i]$)
>   Remove the item at the given position in the list, and return it. If no index is specified, a.pop() removes and returns the last item in the list. (The square brackets around the i in the method signature denote that the parameter is optional, not that you should type square brackets at that position. You will see this notation frequently in the *Python Library Reference Manual.*)

index(x)
>   Return the index in the list of the first item whose value is x. It is an error if there is no such item.

count(x)
>   Return the number of times x appears in the list.

```
sort()
```
    Sort the items of the list, in place.

```
reverse()
```
    Reverse the elements of the list, in place.

An example that uses most of the list methods:

```
>>> a = [66.25, 333, 333, 1, 1234.5]
>>> print a.count(333), a.count(66.25), a.count('x')
2 1 0
>>> a.insert(2, -1)
>>> a.append(333)
>>> a
[66.25, 333, -1, 333, 1, 1234.5, 333]
>>> a.index(333)
1
>>> a.remove(333)
>>> a
[66.25, -1, 333, 1, 1234.5, 333]
>>> a.reverse()
>>> a
[333, 1234.5, 1, 333, -1, 66.25]
>>> a.sort()
>>> a
[-1, 1, 66.25, 333, 333, 1234.5]
```

5.1.1 Using Lists as Stacks

The list methods make it very easy to use a list as a stack, where the last element added is the first element retrieved ("last-in, first-out"). To add an item to the top of the stack, use append(). To retrieve an item from the top of the stack, use pop() without an explicit index. For example:

```
>>> stack = [3, 4, 5]
>>> stack.append(6)
>>> stack.append(7)
>>> stack
[3, 4, 5, 6, 7]
>>> stack.pop()
7
>>> stack
[3, 4, 5, 6]
>>> stack.pop()
6
```

```
>>> stack.pop()
5
>>> stack
[3, 4]
```

5.1.2   Using Lists as Queues

You can also use a list conveniently as a queue, where the first element added is the first element retrieved ("first-in, first-out"). To add an item to the back of the queue, use append(). To retrieve an item from the front of the queue, use pop() with 0 as the index. For example:

```
>>> queue = ["Eric", "John", "Michael"]
>>> queue.append("Terry")          # Terry arrives
>>> queue.append("Graham")         # Graham arrives
>>> queue.pop(0)
'Eric'
>>> queue.pop(0)
'John'
>>> queue
['Michael', 'Terry', 'Graham']
```

5.1.3   Functional Programming Tools

There are three built-in functions that are very useful when used with lists: filter(), map(), and reduce().

'filter(*function*, *sequence*)' returns a sequence consisting of those items from the sequence for which *function*(*item*) is true. If *sequence* is a string or tuple, the result will be of the same type; otherwise, it is always a list. For example, to compute some primes:

```
>>> def f(x): return x % 2 != 0 and x % 3 != 0
...
>>> filter(f, range(2, 25))
[5, 7, 11, 13, 17, 19, 23]
```

'map(*function*, *sequence*)' calls *function*(*item*) for each of the items in the sequence and returns a list of the return values. For example, to compute some cubes:

```
>>> def cube(x): return x*x*x
...
>>> map(cube, range(1, 11))
[1, 8, 27, 64, 125, 216, 343, 512, 729, 1000]
```

More than one sequence may be passed; the function must then have as
many arguments as there are sequences and is called with the corresponding item from each sequence (or None if some sequence is shorter than
another). For example:

```
>>> seq = range(8)
>>> def add(x, y): return x+y
...
>>> map(add, seq, seq)
[0, 2, 4, 6, 8, 10, 12, 14]
```

'reduce(*function*, *sequence*)' returns a single value constructed by calling the binary function *function* on the first two items of the sequence,
then on the result and the next item, and so on. For example, to compute
the sum of the numbers 1 through 10:

```
>>> def add(x,y): return x+y
...
>>> reduce(add, range(1, 11))
55
```

If there's only one item in the sequence, its value is returned; if the sequence is empty, an exception is raised.

A third argument can be passed to indicate the starting value. In this case
the starting value is returned for an empty sequence, and the function is
first applied to the starting value and the first sequence item, then to the
result and the next item, and so on. For example,

```
>>> def sum(seq):
...     def add(x,y): return x+y
...     return reduce(add, seq, 0)
...
>>> sum(range(1, 11))
55
>>> sum([])
0
```

Don't use this example's definition of sum(): since summing numbers is
such a common need, a built-in function sum(*sequence*) is already provided, and works exactly like this.[1]

---

[1] Added in version 2.3.

5.1.4   List Comprehensions

List comprehensions provide a concise way to create lists without resorting to use of map(), filter() and/or lambda. The resulting list definition tends often to be clearer than lists built using those constructs. Each list comprehension consists of an expression followed by a for clause, then zero or more for or if clauses. The result will be a list resulting from evaluating the expression in the context of the for and if clauses which follow it. If the expression would evaluate to a tuple, it must be parenthesized.

```
>>> freshfruit = [' banana', ' loganberry ', 'plum  ']
>>> [weapon.strip() for weapon in freshfruit]
['banana', 'loganberry', 'plum']
>>> vec = [2, 4, 6]
>>> [3*x for x in vec]
[6, 12, 18]
>>> [3*x for x in vec if x > 3]
[12, 18]
>>> [3*x for x in vec if x < 2]
[]
>>> [[x,x**2] for x in vec]
[[2, 4], [4, 16], [6, 36]]
>>> [x, x**2 for x in vec] # error - need () for tuples
  File "<stdin>", line 1, in ?
    [x, x**2 for x in vec]
              ^
SyntaxError: invalid syntax
>>> [(x, x**2) for x in vec]
[(2, 4), (4, 16), (6, 36)]
>>> vec1 = [2, 4, 6]
>>> vec2 = [4, 3, -9]
>>> [x*y for x in vec1 for y in vec2]
[8, 6, -18, 16, 12, -36, 24, 18, -54]
>>> [x+y for x in vec1 for y in vec2]
[6, 5, -7, 8, 7, -5, 10, 9, -3]
>>> [vec1[i]*vec2[i] for i in range(len(vec1))]
[8, 12, -54]
```

List comprehensions are much more flexible than map() and can be applied to complex expressions and nested functions:

```
>>> [str(round(355/113.0, i)) for i in range(1,6)]
['3.1', '3.14', '3.142', '3.1416', '3.14159']
```

5.2 The del statement

There is a way to remove an item from a list given its index instead of its value: the del statement. This differs from the pop() method which returns a value. The del statement can also be used to remove slices from a list or clear the entire list (which we did earlier by assignment of an empty list to the slice). For example:

```
>>> a = [-1, 1, 66.25, 333, 333, 1234.5]
>>> del a[0]
>>> a
[1, 66.25, 333, 333, 1234.5]
>>> del a[2:4]
>>> a
[1, 66.25, 1234.5]
>>> del a[:]
>>> a
[]
```

del can also be used to delete entire variables:

```
>>> del a
```

Referencing the name a hereafter is an error (at least until another value is assigned to it). We'll find other uses for del later.

5.3 Tuples and Sequences

We saw that lists and strings have many common properties, such as indexing and slicing operations. They are two examples of *sequence* data types. Since Python is an evolving language, other sequence data types may be added. There is also another standard sequence data type: the *tuple*.

A tuple consists of a number of values separated by commas, for instance:

```
>>> t = 12345, 54321, 'hello!'
>>> t[0]
12345
>>> t
(12345, 54321, 'hello!')
>>> # Tuples may be nested:
... u = t, (1, 2, 3, 4, 5)
```

```
>>> u
((12345, 54321, 'hello!'), (1, 2, 3, 4, 5))
```

As you see, on output tuples are always enclosed in parentheses, so that nested tuples are interpreted correctly; they may be input with or without surrounding parentheses, although often parentheses are necessary anyway (if the tuple is part of a larger expression).

Tuples have many uses. For example: (x, y) coordinate pairs, employee records from a database, etc. Tuples, like strings, are immutable: it is not possible to assign to the individual items of a tuple (you can simulate much of the same effect with slicing and concatenation, though). It is also possible to create tuples which contain mutable objects, such as lists.

A special problem is the construction of tuples containing 0 or 1 items: the syntax has some extra quirks to accommodate these. Empty tuples are constructed by an empty pair of parentheses; a tuple with one item is constructed by following a value with a comma (it is not sufficient to enclose a single value in parentheses). Ugly, but effective. For example:

```
>>> empty = ()
>>> singleton = 'hello',    # <-- note trailing comma
>>> len(empty)
0
>>> len(singleton)
1
>>> singleton
('hello',)
```

The statement t = 12345, 54321, 'hello!' is an example of *tuple packing*: the values 12345, 54321 and 'hello!' are packed together in a tuple. The reverse operation is also possible:

```
>>> x, y, z = t
```

This is called, appropriately enough, *sequence unpacking*. Sequence unpacking requires the list of variables on the left to have the same number of elements as the length of the sequence. Note that multiple assignment is really just a combination of tuple packing and sequence unpacking!

There is a small bit of asymmetry here: packing multiple values always creates a tuple, and unpacking works for any sequence.

5.4 Sets

Python also includes a data type for *sets*. A set is an unordered collection with no duplicate elements. Basic uses include membership testing and eliminating duplicate entries. Set objects also support mathematical operations like union, intersection, difference, and symmetric difference.

Here is a brief demonstration:

```
>>> basket = ['apple', 'orange', 'apple', 'pear',
              'orange', 'banana']
>>> fruit = set(basket)  # make set without duplicates
>>> fruit
set(['orange', 'pear', 'apple', 'banana'])
>>> 'orange' in fruit    # fast membership testing
True
>>> 'crabgrass' in fruit
False

>>> # Demonstrate set operations on unique letters
    # from two words
...
>>> a = set('abracadabra')
>>> b = set('alacazam')
>>> a       # unique letters in a
set(['a', 'r', 'b', 'c', 'd'])
>>> a - b  # letters in a but not in b
set(['r', 'd', 'b'])
>>> a | b  # letters in either a or b
set(['a', 'c', 'r', 'd', 'b', 'm', 'z', 'l'])
>>> a & b  # letters in both a and b
set(['a', 'c'])
>>> a ^ b  # letters in a or b but not both
set(['r', 'd', 'b', 'm', 'z', 'l'])
```

5.5 Dictionaries

Another useful data type built into Python is the *dictionary*. Dictionaries are sometimes found in other languages as "associative arrays" or "hashes". Unlike sequences, which are indexed by a range of numbers, dictionaries are indexed by *keys*, which can be any immutable type; strings and numbers can always be keys. Tuples can be used as keys if they contain only strings, numbers, or tuples; if a tuple contains any mutable object either directly or indirectly, it cannot be used as a key. You can't use lists as keys, since lists can be modified in place using index assignments, slice assignments, or methods like append() and extend().

It is best to think of a dictionary as an unordered set of *key: value* pairs, with the requirement that the keys are unique (within one dictionary). A pair of braces creates an empty dictionary: {}. Placing a comma-separated list of key:value pairs within the braces adds initial key:value pairs to the dictionary; this is also the way dictionaries are written on output.

The main operations on a dictionary are storing a value with some key and extracting the value given the key. It is also possible to delete a key:value pair with del. If you store using a key that is already in use, the old value associated with that key is forgotten. It is an error to extract a value using a non-existent key.

The keys() method of a dictionary object returns a list of all the keys used in the dictionary, in arbitrary order (if you want it sorted, just apply the sort() method to the list of keys). To check whether a single key is in the dictionary, either use the dictionary's has_key() method or the in keyword.

Here is a small example using a dictionary:

```
>>> tel = {'jack': 4098, 'sape': 4139}
>>> tel['guido'] = 4127
>>> tel
{'sape': 4139, 'guido': 4127, 'jack': 4098}
>>> tel['jack']
4098
>>> del tel['sape']
>>> tel['irv'] = 4127
>>> tel
{'guido': 4127, 'irv': 4127, 'jack': 4098}
>>> tel.keys()
['guido', 'irv', 'jack']
>>> tel.has_key('guido')
True
>>> 'guido' in tel
True
```

The dict() constructor builds dictionaries directly from lists of key-value pairs stored as tuples. When the pairs form a pattern, list comprehensions can compactly specify the key-value list.

```
>>> dict([('sape', 4139), ('guido', 4127),
          ('jack', 4098)])
{'sape': 4139, 'jack': 4098, 'guido': 4127}
>>> dict([(x, x**2) for x in (2, 4, 6)]) # use a list
                                         # comprehension
{2: 4, 4: 16, 6: 36}
```

Later in the tutorial, we will learn about *generator expressions* which are even better suited for the task of supplying key-value pairs to the dict() constructor.

When the keys are simple strings, it is sometimes easier to specify pairs using keyword arguments:

```
>>> dict(sape=4139, guido=4127, jack=4098)
{'sape': 4139, 'jack': 4098, 'guido': 4127}
```

5.6 Looping Techniques

When looping through dictionaries, the key and corresponding value can be retrieved at the same time using the iteritems() method.

```
>>> knights = {'gallahad': 'pure', 'robin': 'brave'}
>>> for k, v in knights.iteritems():
...     print k, 'the', v
...
gallahad the pure
robin the brave
```

When looping through a sequence, the position index and corresponding value can be retrieved at the same time using the enumerate() function.

```
>>> for i, v in enumerate(['tic', 'tac', 'toe']):
...     print i, v
...
0 tic
1 tac
2 toe
```

To loop over two or more sequences at the same time, the entries can be paired with the zip() function.

```
>>> questions = ['name', 'quest', 'favorite color']
>>> answers = ['lancelot', 'the holy grail', 'blue']
>>> for q, a in zip(questions, answers):
...         print 'What is your %s?  It is %s.' % (q, a)
...
What is your name?  It is lancelot.
What is your quest?  It is the holy grail.
What is your favorite color?  It is blue.
```

To loop over a sequence in reverse, first specify the sequence in a forward direction and then call the reversed() function.

```
>>> for i in reversed(xrange(1,10,2)):
...         print i
...
9
7
5
3
1
```

To loop over a sequence in sorted order, use the sorted() function which returns a new sorted list while leaving the source unaltered.

```
>>> basket = ['apple', 'orange', 'apple', 'pear',
              'orange', 'banana']
>>> for f in sorted(set(basket)):
...         print f
...
apple
banana
orange
pear
```

5.7   More on Conditions

The conditions used in while and if statements can contain any operators, not just comparisons.

The comparison operators in and not in check whether a value occurs (or does not occur) in a sequence. The operators is and is not compare whether two objects are really the same object; this only matters for mutable objects like lists. All comparison operators have the same priority, which is lower than that of all numerical operators.

Comparisons can be chained. For example, a < b == c tests whether a is less than b and moreover b equals c.

Comparisons may be combined using the Boolean operators and and or, and the outcome of a comparison (or of any other Boolean expression) may be negated with not. These have lower priorities than comparison operators; between them, not has the highest priority and or the lowest, so that A and not B or C is equivalent to (A and (not B)) or C. As always, parentheses can be used to express the desired composition.

The Boolean operators and and or are so-called *short-circuit* operators: their arguments are evaluated from left to right, and evaluation stops as soon as the outcome is determined. For example, if A and C are true but B is false, A and B and C does not evaluate the expression C. When used as a general value and not as a Boolean, the return value of a short-circuit operator is the last evaluated argument.

It is possible to assign the result of a comparison or other Boolean expression to a variable. For example,

```
>>> str1, str2, str3 = '', 'Trondheim', 'Hammer Dance'
>>> non_null = str1 or str2 or str3
>>> non_null
'Trondheim'
```

Note that in Python, unlike C, assignment cannot occur inside expressions. C programmers may grumble about this, but it avoids a common class of problems encountered in C programs: typing = in an expression when == was intended.

5.8   Comparing Sequences and Other Types

Sequence objects may be compared to other objects with the same sequence type. The comparison uses *lexicographical* ordering: first the first two items are compared, and if they differ this determines the outcome of the comparison; if they are equal, the next two items are compared, and so on, until either sequence is exhausted. If two items to be compared are themselves sequences of the same type, the lexicographical comparison is carried out recursively. If all items of two sequences compare equal, the sequences are considered equal. If one sequence is an initial sub-sequence of the other, the shorter sequence is the smaller (lesser) one. Lexicographical ordering for strings uses the ASCII ordering for individual characters. Some examples of comparisons between sequences of the same type:

```
(1, 2, 3)               < (1, 2, 4)
[1, 2, 3]               < [1, 2, 4]
'ABC' < 'C' < 'Pascal' < 'Python'
(1, 2, 3, 4)           < (1, 2, 4)
(1, 2)                 < (1, 2, -1)
(1, 2, 3)             == (1.0, 2.0, 3.0)
(1, 2, ('aa', 'ab'))   < (1, 2, ('abc', 'a'), 4)
```

Note that comparing objects of different types is legal. The outcome is deterministic but arbitrary: the types are ordered by their name. Thus, a list is always smaller than a string, a string is always smaller than a tuple, etc.[2] Mixed numeric types are compared according to their numeric value, so 0 equals 0.0, etc.

---

[2]The rules for comparing objects of different types should not be relied upon; they may change in a future version of the language.

6 Modules

If you quit from the Python interpreter and enter it again, the definitions you have made (functions and variables) are lost. Therefore, if you want to write a somewhat longer program, you are better off using a text editor to prepare the input for the interpreter and running it with that file as input instead. This is known as creating a *script*. As your program gets longer, you may want to split it into several files for easier maintenance. You may also want to use a handy function that you've written in several programs without copying its definition into each program.

To support this, Python has a way to put definitions in a file and use them in a script or in an interactive instance of the interpreter. Such a file is called a *module*; definitions from a module can be *imported* into other modules or into the *main* module (the collection of variables that you have access to in a script executed at the top level and in calculator mode).

A module is a file containing Python definitions and statements. The file name is the module name with the suffix '.py' appended. Within a module, the module's name (as a string) is available as the value of the global variable __name__. For instance, use your favorite text editor to create a file called 'fibo.py' in the current directory with the following contents:

```
# Fibonacci numbers module

def fib(n):    # write Fibonacci series up to n
    a, b = 0, 1
    while b < n:
        print b,
        a, b = b, a+b

def fib2(n):   # return Fibonacci series up to n
    result = []
    a, b = 0, 1
    while b < n:
        result.append(b)
        a, b = b, a+b
    return result
```

Now enter the Python interpreter and import this module with the following command:

```
>>> import fibo
```

This does not enter the names of the functions defined in fibo directly in the current symbol table; it only enters the module name fibo there. Using the module name you can access the functions:

```
>>> fibo.fib(1000)
1 1 2 3 5 8 13 21 34 55 89 144 233 377 610 987
>>> fibo.fib2(100)
[1, 1, 2, 3, 5, 8, 13, 21, 34, 55, 89]
>>> fibo.__name__
'fibo'
```

If you intend to use a function often you can assign it to a local name:

```
>>> fib = fibo.fib
>>> fib(500)
1 1 2 3 5 8 13 21 34 55 89 144 233 377
```

6.1   More on Modules

A module can contain executable statements as well as function definitions. These statements are intended to initialize the module. They are executed only the *first* time the module is imported somewhere.[1]

Each module has its own private symbol table, which is used as the global symbol table by all functions defined in the module. Thus, the author of a module can use global variables in the module without worrying about accidental clashes with a user's global variables. On the other hand, if you know what you are doing you can touch a module's global variables with the same notation used to refer to its functions, modname.itemname.

Modules can import other modules. It is customary but not required to place all import statements at the beginning of a module (or script, for that matter). The imported module names are placed in the importing module's global symbol table.

There is a variant of the import statement that imports names from a module directly into the importing module's symbol table. For example:

---

[1]In fact function definitions are also 'statements' that are 'executed'; the execution enters the function name in the module's global symbol table.

```
>>> from fibo import fib, fib2
>>> fib(500)
1 1 2 3 5 8 13 21 34 55 89 144 233 377
```

This does not introduce the module name from which the imports are taken in the local symbol table (so in the example, fibo is not defined).

There is even a variant to import all names that a module defines:

```
>>> from fibo import *
>>> fib(500)
1 1 2 3 5 8 13 21 34 55 89 144 233 377
```

This imports all names except those beginning with an underscore (_).

6.1.1   The Module Search Path

When a module named spam is imported, the interpreter searches for a file named 'spam.py' in the current directory, and then in the list of directories specified by the environment variable PYTHONPATH. This has the same syntax as the shell variable PATH, that is, a list of directory names. When PYTHONPATH is not set, or when the file is not found there, the search continues in an installation-dependent default path; on UNIX, this is usually '.:/usr/local/lib/python'.

Actually, modules are searched for in the list of directories given by the variable sys.path which is initialized from the directory containing the input script (or the current directory), PYTHONPATH and the installation-dependent default. This allows Python programs that know what they're doing to modify or replace the module search path. Note that because the directory containing the script being run is on the search path, it is important that the script not have the same name as a standard module, or Python will attempt to load the script as a module when that module is imported. This will generally be an error. See section 6.2, "Standard Modules," for more information.

6.1.2   "Compiled" Python files

As an important speed-up of the start-up time for short programs that use a lot of standard modules, if a file called 'spam.pyc' exists in the directory where 'spam.py' is found, this is assumed to contain an already-"byte-compiled" version of the module spam. The modification time of the version of 'spam.py' used to create 'spam.pyc' is recorded in 'spam.pyc', and the '.pyc' file is ignored if these don't match.

Normally, you don't need to do anything to create the 'spam.pyc' file. Whenever 'spam.py' is successfully compiled, an attempt is made to write the compiled version to 'spam.pyc'. It is not an error if this attempt fails; if for any reason the file is not written completely, the resulting 'spam.pyc' file will be recognized as invalid and thus ignored later. The contents of the 'spam.pyc' file are platform independent, so a Python module directory can be shared by machines of different architectures.

Some tips for experts:

- When the Python interpreter is invoked with the -O flag, optimized code is generated and stored in '.pyo' files. The optimizer currently doesn't help much; it only removes assert statements. When -O is used, *all* bytecode is optimized; .pyc files are ignored and .py files are compiled to optimized bytecode.

- Passing two -O flags to the Python interpreter (-OO) will cause the bytecode compiler to perform optimizations that could in some rare cases result in malfunctioning programs. Currently only __doc__ strings are removed from the bytecode, resulting in more compact '.pyo' files. Since some programs may rely on having these available, you should only use this option if you know what you're doing.

- A program doesn't run any faster when it is read from a '.pyc' or '.pyo' file than when it is read from a '.py' file; the only thing that's faster about '.pyc' or '.pyo' files is the speed with which they are loaded.

- When a script is run by giving its name on the command line, the bytecode for the script is never written to a '.pyc' or '.pyo' file. Thus, the startup time of a script may be reduced by moving most of its code to a module and having a small bootstrap script that imports that module. It is also possible to name a '.pyc' or '.pyo' file directly on the command line.

- The module compileall can create '.pyc' files (or '.pyo' files when -O is used) for all modules in a directory.

6.2   Standard Modules

Python comes with a library of standard modules, described in a separate document, the *Python Library Reference Manual*. Some modules are built into the interpreter; these provide access to operations that are not part of the core of the language but are nevertheless built in, either for efficiency or to provide access to operating system primitives such as system calls.

The set of such modules is a configuration option which also depends on the underlying platform. For example, the posix module is only provided on UNIX systems. One particular module deserves some attention: sys, which is built into every Python interpreter. The variables sys.ps1 and sys.ps2 define the strings used as primary and secondary prompts:

```
>>> import sys
>>> sys.ps1
'>>> '
>>> sys.ps2
'... '
>>> sys.ps1 = 'C> '
C> print 'Yuck!'
Yuck!
C>
```

These two variables are only defined if the interpreter is in interactive mode.

The variable sys.path is a list of strings that determines the interpreter's search path for modules. It is initialized to a default path taken from the environment variable PYTHONPATH, or from a built-in default if this is not set. You can modify it using standard list operations:

```
>>> import sys
>>> sys.path.append('/ufs/guido/lib/python')
```

6.3 The dir() Function

The built-in function dir() is used to find out which names a module defines. It returns a sorted list of strings:

```
>>> import fibo, sys
>>> dir(fibo)
['__name__', 'fib', 'fib2']
>>> dir(sys)
['__displayhook__', '__doc__', '__excepthook__',
 '__name__', '__stderr__', '__stdin__', '__stdout__',
 '_getframe', 'api_version', 'argv',
 'builtin_module_names', 'byteorder', 'callstats',
 'copyright', 'displayhook', 'exc_clear', 'exc_info',
 'exc_type', 'excepthook', 'exec_prefix', 'executable',
 'exit', 'getdefaultencoding', 'getdlopenflags',
```

```
'getrecursionlimit', 'getrefcount', 'hexversion',
'maxint', 'maxunicode', 'meta_path', 'modules', 'path',
'path_hooks', 'path_importer_cache', 'platform',
'prefix', 'ps1', 'ps2', 'setcheckinterval',
'setdlopenflags', 'setprofile', 'setrecursionlimit',
'settrace', 'stderr', 'stdin', 'stdout', 'version',
'version_info', 'warnoptions']
```

Without arguments, dir() lists the names you have defined currently:

```
>>> a = [1, 2, 3, 4, 5]
>>> import fibo
>>> fib = fibo.fib
>>> dir()
['__builtins__', '__doc__', '__file__', '__name__', 'a',
'fib', 'fibo', 'sys']
```

Note that it lists all types of names: variables, modules, functions, etc.

dir() does not list the names of built-in functions and variables. If you want a list of those, they are defined in the standard module __builtin__:

```
>>> import __builtin__
>>> dir(__builtin__)
['ArithmeticError', 'AssertionError', 'AttributeError',
'DeprecationWarning', 'EOFError', 'Ellipsis',
'EnvironmentError', 'Exception', 'False',
'FloatingPointError', 'FutureWarning', 'IOError',
'ImportError', 'IndentationError', 'IndexError',
'KeyError', 'KeyboardInterrupt', 'LookupError',
'MemoryError', 'NameError', 'None', 'NotImplemented',
'NotImplementedError', 'OSError', 'OverflowError',
'PendingDeprecationWarning', 'ReferenceError',
'RuntimeError', 'RuntimeWarning', 'StandardError',
'StopIteration', 'SyntaxError', 'SyntaxWarning',
'SystemError', 'SystemExit', 'TabError', 'True',
'TypeError', 'UnboundLocalError', 'UnicodeDecodeError',
'UnicodeEncodeError', 'UnicodeError',
'UnicodeTranslateError', 'UserWarning', 'ValueError',
'Warning', 'WindowsError', 'ZeroDivisionError', '_',
'__debug__', '__doc__', '__import__', '__name__', 'abs',
'apply', 'basestring', 'bool', 'buffer', 'callable',
'chr', 'classmethod', 'cmp', 'coerce', 'compile',
'complex', 'copyright', 'credits', 'delattr', 'dict',
```

```
'dir', 'divmod', 'enumerate', 'eval', 'execfile',
'exit', 'file', 'filter', 'float', 'frozenset',
'getattr', 'globals', 'hasattr', 'hash', 'help', 'hex',
'id', 'input', 'int', 'intern', 'isinstance',
'issubclass', 'iter', 'len', 'license', 'list',
'locals', 'long', 'map', 'max', 'min', 'object', 'oct',
'open', 'ord', 'pow', 'property', 'quit', 'range',
'raw_input', 'reduce', 'reload', 'repr', 'reversed',
'round', 'set', 'setattr', 'slice', 'sorted',
'staticmethod', 'str', 'sum', 'super', 'tuple', 'type',
'unichr', 'unicode', 'vars', 'xrange', 'zip']
```

6.4 Packages

Packages are a way of structuring Python's module namespace by using "dotted module names". For example, the module name A.B designates a submodule named 'B' in a package named 'A'. Just like the use of modules saves the authors of different modules from having to worry about each other's global variable names, the use of dotted module names saves the authors of multi-module packages like NumPy or the Python Imaging Library from having to worry about each other's module names.

Suppose you want to design a collection of modules (a "package") for the uniform handling of sound files and sound data. There are many different sound file formats (usually recognized by their extension, for example: '.wav', '.aiff', '.au'), so you may need to create and maintain a growing collection of modules for the conversion between the various file formats. There are also many different operations you might want to perform on sound data (such as mixing, adding echo, applying an equalizer function, creating an artificial stereo effect), so in addition you will be writing a never-ending stream of modules to perform these operations. Here's a possible structure for your package (expressed in terms of a hierarchical filesystem):

```
Sound/                          Top-level package
    __init__.py         Initialize the sound package
    Formats/            Subpackage for file formats
        __init__.py
        wavread.py
        wavwrite.py
        aiffread.py
        aiffwrite.py
        auread.py
        auwrite.py
```

```
                . . .
    Effects/              Subpackage for sound effects
           __init__.py
           echo.py
           surround.py
           reverse.py
                . . .
    Filters/                   Subpackage for filters
           __init__.py
           equalizer.py
           vocoder.py
           karaoke.py
                . . .
```

When importing the package, Python searches through the directories on sys.path looking for the package subdirectory.

The '__init__.py' files are required to make Python treat the directories as containing packages; this is done to prevent directories with a common name, such as 'string', from unintentionally hiding valid modules that occur later on the module search path. In the simplest case, '__init__ .py' can just be an empty file, but it can also execute initialization code for the package or set the __all__ variable, described later.

Users of the package can import individual modules from the package, for example:

```
    import Sound.Effects.echo
```

This loads the submodule Sound.Effects.echo. It must be referenced with its full name.

```
    Sound.Effects.echo.echofilter(input, output, delay=0.7,
                                  atten=4)
```

An alternative way of importing the submodule is:

```
    from Sound.Effects import echo
```

This also loads the submodule echo, and makes it available without its package prefix, so it can be used as follows:

```
    echo.echofilter(input, output, delay=0.7, atten=4)
```

Yet another variation is to import the desired function or variable directly:

```
from Sound.Effects.echo import echofilter
```

Again, this loads the submodule echo, but this makes its function
echofilter() directly available:

```
echofilter(input, output, delay=0.7, atten=4)
```

Note that when using from *package* import *item*, the item can be either a submodule (or subpackage) of the package, or some other name
defined in the package, like a function, class or variable. The import
statement first tests whether the item is defined in the package; if not,
it assumes it is a module and attempts to load it. If it fails to find it,
an ImportError exception is raised. Contrarily, when using syntax like
import *item.subitem.subsubitem*, each item except for the last must be a
package; the last item can be a module or a package but can't be a class
or function or variable defined in the previous item.

6.4.1 Importing * From a Package

Now what happens when the user writes from Sound.Effects import
*? Ideally, one would hope that this somehow goes out to the filesystem,
finds which submodules are present in the package, and imports them
all. Unfortunately, this operation does not work very well on Mac and
Windows platforms, where the filesystem does not always have accurate
information about the case of a filename! On these platforms, there is no
guaranteed way to know whether a file 'ECHO.PY' should be imported as a
module echo, Echo or ECHO. (For example, Windows 95 has the annoying
practice of showing all file names with a capitalized first letter.) The DOS
8+3 filename restriction adds another interesting problem for long module
names.

The only solution is for the package author to provide an explicit index
of the package. The import statement uses the following convention: if a
package's '__init__.py' code defines a list named __all__, it is taken
to be the list of module names that should be imported when from *package* import * is encountered. It is up to the package author to keep
this list up-to-date when a new version of the package is released. Package authors may also decide not to support it, if they don't see a use for
importing * from their package. For example, the file 'Sounds/Effects/_
_init__.py' could contain the following code:

```
__all__ = ["echo", "surround", "reverse"]
```

This would mean that from Sound.Effects import * would import the
three named submodules of the Sound package.

If __all__ is not defined, the statement from Sound.Effects import
* does *not* import all submodules from the package Sound.Effects into
the current namespace; it only ensures that the package Sound.Effects
has been imported (possibly running any initialization code in '__init__
.py') and then imports whatever names are defined in the package. This
includes any names defined (and submodules explicitly loaded) by '__
init__.py'. It also includes any submodules of the package that were
explicitly loaded by previous import statements. Consider this code:

```
import Sound.Effects.echo
import Sound.Effects.surround
from Sound.Effects import *
```

In this example, the echo and surround modules are imported in the current namespace because they are defined in the Sound.Effects package
when the from...import statement is executed. (This also works when
__all__ is defined.)

Note that in general the practice of importing * from a module or package
is frowned upon, since it often causes poorly readable code. However, it is
okay to use it to save typing in interactive sessions, and certain modules
are designed to export only names that follow certain patterns.

Remember, there is nothing wrong with using from Package import
specific_submodule! In fact, this is the recommended notation unless
the importing module needs to use submodules with the same name from
different packages.

6.4.2   Intra-package References

The submodules often need to refer to each other. For example, the
surround module might use the echo module. In fact, such references are
so common that the import statement first looks in the containing package
before looking in the standard module search path. Thus, the surround
module can simply use import echo or from echo import echofilter.
If the imported module is not found in the current package (the package
of which the current module is a submodule), the import statement looks
for a top-level module with the given name.

When packages are structured into subpackages (as with the Sound package in the example), there's no shortcut to refer to submodules of sibling
packages—the full name of the subpackage must be used. For example, if
the module Sound.Filters.vocoder needs to use the echo module in the
Sound.Effects package, it can use from Sound.Effects import echo.

Starting with Python 2.5, in addition to the implicit relative imports described above, you can write explicit relative imports with the from module import name form of import statement. These explicit relative imports use leading dots to indicate the current and parent packages involved in the relative import. From the surround module for example, you might use:

```
from . import echo
from .. import Formats
from ..Filters import equalizer
```

Note that both explicit and implicit relative imports are based on the name of the current module. Since the name of the main module is always "__main__", modules intended for use as the main module of a Python application should always use absolute imports.

6.4.3 Packages in Multiple Directories

Packages support one more special attribute, __path__. This is initialized to be a list containing the name of the directory holding the package's '__init__.py' before the code in that file is executed. This variable can be modified; doing so affects future searches for modules and subpackages contained in the package.

While this feature is not often needed, it can be used to extend the set of modules found in a package.

7 Input and Output

There are several ways to present the output of a program; data can be printed in a human-readable form, or written to a file for future use. This chapter will discuss some of the possibilities.

7.1 Fancier Output Formatting

So far we've encountered two ways of writing values: *expression statements* and the `print` statement. (A third way is using the `write()` method of file objects; the standard output file can be referenced as `sys.stdout`. See the *Python Library Reference Manual* for more information on this.)

Often you'll want more control over the formatting of your output than simply printing space-separated values. There are two ways to format your output; the first way is to do all the string handling yourself; using string slicing and concatenation operations you can create any layout you can imagine. The standard module `string` contains some useful operations for padding strings to a given column width; these will be discussed shortly. The second way is to use the `%` operator with a string as the left argument. The `%` operator interprets the left argument much like a `sprintf()`-style format string to be applied to the right argument, and returns the string resulting from this formatting operation.

One question remains, of course: how do you convert values to strings? Luckily, Python has ways to convert any value to a string: pass it to the `repr()` or `str()` functions. Reverse quotes (` `` `) are equivalent to `repr()`, but they are no longer used in modern Python code and will likely not be in future versions of the language.

The `str()` function is meant to return representations of values which are fairly human-readable, while `repr()` is meant to generate representations which can be read by the interpreter (or will force a `SyntaxError` if there is not equivalent syntax). For objects which don't have a particular representation for human consumption, `str()` will return the same value as `repr()`. Many values, such as numbers or structures like lists and dictionaries, have the same representation using either function. Strings and floating point numbers, in particular, have two distinct representations.

Some examples:

```
>>> s = 'Hello, world.'
>>> str(s)
'Hello, world.'
>>> repr(s)
"'Hello, world.'"
>>> str(0.1)
'0.1'
>>> repr(0.1)
'0.10000000000000001'
>>> x = 10 * 3.25
>>> y = 200 * 200
>>> s = 'The value of x is ' + repr(x) + ', and y is '
    + repr(y)
>>> print s
The value of x is 32.5, and y is 40000
>>> # The repr() of a string adds quotes and backslashes:
... hello = 'hello, world\n'
>>> hellos = repr(hello)
>>> print hellos
'hello, world\n'
>>> # The argument to repr() may be any Python object:
... repr((x, y, ('spam', 'eggs')))
"(32.5, 40000, ('spam', 'eggs'))"
>>> # reverse quotes are convenient in interactive
 sessions:
... `x, y, ('spam', 'eggs')`
"(32.5, 40000, ('spam', 'eggs'))"
```

Here are two ways to write a table of squares and cubes:

```
>>> for x in range(1, 11):
...     print repr(x).rjust(2),
...     print repr(x*x).rjust(3),
...     # Note trailing comma on previous lines
...     print repr(x*x*x).rjust(4)
...
 1   1    1
 2   4    8
 3   9   27
 4  16   64
 5  25  125
 6  36  216
 7  49  343
 8  64  512
```

```
 9  81  729
10 100 1000
>>> for x in range(1,11):
...     print '%2d %3d %4d' % (x, x*x, x*x*x)
...
 1   1    1
 2   4    8
 3   9   27
 4  16   64
 5  25  125
 6  36  216
 7  49  343
 8  64  512
 9  81  729
10 100 1000
```

(Note that one space between each column was added by the way print works: it always adds spaces between its arguments.)

This example demonstrates the rjust() method of string objects, which right-justifies a string in a field of a given width by padding it with spaces on the left. There are similar methods ljust() and center(). These methods do not write anything, they just return a new string. If the input string is too long, they don't truncate it, but return it unchanged; this will mess up your column lay-out but that's usually better than the alternative, which would be lying about a value. (If you really want truncation you can always add a slice operation, as in 'x.ljust(n)[:n]'.)

There is another method, zfill(), which pads a numeric string on the left with zeros. It understands about plus and minus signs:

```
>>> '12'.zfill(5)
'00012'
>>> '-3.14'.zfill(7)
'-003.14'
>>> '3.14159265359'.zfill(5)
'3.14159265359'
```

Using the % operator looks like this:

```
>>> import math
>>> print 'PI is approximately %5.3f.' % math.pi
PI is approximately 3.142.
```

If there is more than one format in the string, you need to pass a tuple as right operand, as in this example:

```
>>> table = {'Sjoerd': 4127, 'Jack': 4098, 'Dcab': 7678}
>>> for name, phone in table.items():
...     print '%-10s ==> %10d' % (name, phone)
...
Jack       ==>        4098
Dcab       ==>        7678
Sjoerd     ==>        4127
```

Most formats work exactly as in C and require that you pass the proper type; however, if you don't you get an exception, not a core dump. The %s format is more relaxed: if the corresponding argument is not a string object, it is converted to a string using the str() built-in function. Using * to pass the width or precision in as a separate (integer) argument is supported. The C formats %n and %p are not supported.

If you have a really long format string that you don't want to split up, it would be nice if you could reference the variables to be formatted by name instead of by position. This can be done by using the form %(name)format, as shown here:

```
>>> table = {'Sjoerd': 4127, 'Jack': 4098, 'Dcab': 7678}
>>> print '%(Jack)d; %(Sjoerd)d; %(Dcab)d' % table
4098; 4127; 7678
```

This is particularly useful in combination with the new built-in vars() function, which returns a dictionary containing all local variables.

7.2   Reading and Writing Files

open() returns a file object, and is most commonly used with two arguments: 'open(*filename*, *mode*)'.

```
>>> f=open('/tmp/workfile', 'w')
>>> print f
<open file '/tmp/workfile', mode 'w' at 80a0960>
```

The first argument is a string containing the filename. The second argument is another string containing a few characters describing the way in which the file will be used. *mode* can be 'r' when the file will only be read, 'w' for only writing (any existing file with the same name will be erased), and 'a' opens the file for appending; any data written to the file is automatically added to the end. 'r+' opens the file for both reading and writing. The *mode* argument is optional; 'r' will be assumed if it's omitted.

On Windows and the Macintosh, 'b' appended to the mode opens the file in binary mode, so there are also modes like 'rb', 'wb', and 'r+b'. Windows makes a distinction between text and binary files; the end-of-line characters in text files are automatically altered slightly when data is read or written. This behind-the-scenes modification to file data is fine for ASCII text files, but it'll corrupt binary data like that in 'JPEG' or 'EXE' files. Be very careful to use binary mode when reading and writing such files.

7.2.1 Methods of File Objects

The rest of the examples in this section will assume that a file object called f has already been created.

To read a file's contents, call f.read(*size*), which reads some quantity of data and returns it as a string. *size* is an optional numeric argument. When *size* is omitted or negative, the entire contents of the file will be read and returned; it's your problem if the file is twice as large as your machine's memory. Otherwise, at most *size* bytes are read and returned. If the end of the file has been reached, f.read() will return an empty string ("").

```
>>> f.read()
'This is the entire file.\n'
>>> f.read()
''
```

f.readline() reads a single line from the file; a newline character (\n) is left at the end of the string, and is only omitted on the last line of the file if the file doesn't end in a newline. This makes the return value unambiguous; if f.readline() returns an empty string, the end of the file has been reached, while a blank line is represented by '\n', a string containing only a single newline.

```
>>> f.readline()
'This is the first line of the file.\n'
>>> f.readline()
'Second line of the file\n'
>>> f.readline()
''
```

f.readlines() returns a list containing all the lines of data in the file. If given an optional parameter *sizehint*, it reads that many bytes from the file and enough more to complete a line, and returns the lines from that. This is often used to allow efficient reading of a large file by lines, but without having to load the entire file in memory. Only complete lines will be returned.

```
>>> f.readlines()
['This is the first line of the file.\n',
 'Second line of the file\n']
```

An alternate approach to reading lines is to loop over the file object. This is memory efficient, fast, and leads to simpler code:

```
>>> for line in f:
        print line,

This is the first line of the file.
Second line of the file
```

The alternative approach is simpler but does not provide as fine-grained control. Since the two approaches manage line buffering differently, they should not be mixed.

f.write(*string*) writes the contents of *string* to the file, returning None.

```
>>> f.write('This is a test\n')
```

To write something other than a string, it needs to be converted to a string first:

```
>>> value = ('the answer', 42)
>>> s = str(value)
>>> f.write(s)
```

f.tell() returns an integer giving the file object's current position in the file, measured in bytes from the beginning of the file. To change the file object's position, use 'f.seek(*offset*, *from_what*)'. The position is computed from adding *offset* to a reference point; the reference point is selected by the *from_what* argument. A *from_what* value of 0 measures from the beginning of the file, 1 uses the current file position, and 2 uses the end of the file as the reference point. *from_what* can be omitted and defaults to 0, using the beginning of the file as the reference point.

```
>>> f = open('/tmp/workfile', 'r+')
>>> f.write('0123456789abcdef')
>>> f.seek(5)     # Go to the 6th byte in the file
>>> f.read(1)
'5'
>>> f.seek(-3, 2) # Go to the 3rd byte before the end
>>> f.read(1)
'd'
```

When you're done with a file, call f.close() to close it and free up any system resources taken up by the open file. After calling f.close(), attempts to use the file object will automatically fail.

```
>>> f.close()
>>> f.read()
Traceback (most recent call last):
  File "<stdin>", line 1, in ?
ValueError: I/O operation on closed file
```

File objects have some additional methods, such as isatty() and truncate() which are less frequently used; consult the *Python Library Reference Manual* for a complete guide to file objects.

7.2.2 The pickle Module

Strings can easily be written to and read from a file. Numbers take a bit more effort, since the read() method only returns strings, which will have to be passed to a function like int(), which takes a string like '123' and returns its numeric value 123. However, when you want to save more complex data types like lists, dictionaries, or class instances, things get a lot more complicated.

Rather than have users be constantly writing and debugging code to save complicated data types, Python provides a standard module called pickle. This is an amazing module that can take almost any Python object (even some forms of Python code!), and convert it to a string representation; this process is called *pickling*. Reconstructing the object from the string representation is called *unpickling*. Between pickling and unpickling, the string representing the object may have been stored in a file or data, or sent over a network connection to some distant machine.

If you have an object x, and a file object f that's been opened for writing, the simplest way to pickle the object takes only one line of code:

```
pickle.dump(x, f)
```

To unpickle the object again, if f is a file object which has been opened for reading:

```
x = pickle.load(f)
```

(There are other variants of this, used when pickling many objects or when you don't want to write the pickled data to a file; consult the complete documentation for pickle in the *Python Library Reference Manual.*)

pickle is the standard way to make Python objects which can be stored and reused by other programs or by a future invocation of the same program; the technical term for this is a *persistent object.* Because pickle is so widely used, many authors who write Python extensions take care to ensure that new data types such as matrices can be properly pickled and unpickled.

8 Errors and Exceptions

Until now error messages haven't been more than mentioned, but if you have tried out the examples you have probably seen some. There are (at least) two distinguishable kinds of errors: *syntax errors* and *exceptions*.

8.1 Syntax Errors

Syntax errors, also known as parsing errors, are perhaps the most common kind of complaint you get while you are still learning Python:

```
>>> while True print 'Hello world'
  File "<stdin>", line 1, in ?
    while True print 'Hello world'
                  ^
SyntaxError: invalid syntax
```

The parser repeats the offending line and displays a little 'arrow' pointing at the earliest point in the line where the error was detected. The error is caused by (or at least detected at) the token *preceding* the arrow: in the example, the error is detected at the keyword print, since a colon (':') is missing before it. The file name and line number are printed so you know where to look in case the input came from a script.

8.2 Exceptions

Even if a statement or expression is syntactically correct, it may cause an error when an attempt is made to execute it. Errors detected during execution are called *exceptions* and are not unconditionally fatal: you will soon learn how to handle them in Python programs. Most exceptions are not handled by programs, however, and result in error messages as shown here:

```
>>> 10 * (1/0)
Traceback (most recent call last):
  File "<stdin>", line 1, in ?
ZeroDivisionError: integer division or modulo by zero
>>> 4 + spam*3
```

```
Traceback (most recent call last):
  File "<stdin>", line 1, in ?
NameError: name 'spam' is not defined
>>> '2' + 2
Traceback (most recent call last):
  File "<stdin>", line 1, in ?
TypeError: cannot concatenate 'str' and 'int' objects
```

The last line of the error message indicates what happened. Exceptions come in different types, and the type is printed as part of the message: the types in the example are ZeroDivisionError, NameError and TypeError. The string printed as the exception type is the name of the built-in exception that occurred. This is true for all built-in exceptions, but need not be true for user-defined exceptions (although it is a useful convention). Standard exception names are built-in identifiers (not reserved keywords).

The rest of the line provides detail based on the type of exception and what caused it.

The preceding part of the error message shows the context where the exception happened, in the form of a stack traceback. In general it contains a stack traceback listing source lines; however, it will not display lines read from standard input.

The *Python Library Reference Manual* lists the built-in exceptions and their meanings.

8.3   Handling Exceptions

It is possible to write programs that handle selected exceptions. Look at the following example, which asks the user for input until a valid integer has been entered, but allows the user to interrupt the program (using Control-C or whatever the operating system supports); note that a user-generated interruption is signalled by raising the KeyboardInterrupt exception.

```
>>> while True:
...     try:
...         x = int(raw_input("Enter a number: "))
...         break
...     except ValueError:
...         print "Not a valid number.  Try again..."
...
```

The try statement works as follows.

- First, the *try clause* (the statement(s) between the `try` and `except` keywords) is executed.

- If no exception occurs, the *except clause* is skipped and execution of the `try` statement is finished.

- If an exception occurs during execution of the try clause, the rest of the clause is skipped. Then if its type matches the exception named after the `except` keyword, the except clause is executed, and then execution continues after the `try` statement.

- If an exception occurs which does not match the exception named in the except clause, it is passed on to outer `try` statements; if no handler is found, it is an *unhandled exception* and execution stops with a message as shown above.

A `try` statement may have more than one except clause, to specify handlers for different exceptions. At most one handler will be executed. Handlers only handle exceptions that occur in the corresponding try clause, not in other handlers of the same `try` statement. An except clause may name multiple exceptions as a parenthesized tuple, for example:

```
... except (RuntimeError, TypeError, NameError):
...     pass
```

The last except clause may omit the exception name(s), to serve as a wildcard. Use this with extreme caution, since it is easy to mask a real programming error in this way! It can also be used to print an error message and then re-raise the exception (allowing a caller to handle the exception as well):

```
import sys

try:
    f = open('myfile.txt')
    s = f.readline()
    i = int(s.strip())
except IOError, (errno, strerror):
    print "I/O error(%s): %s" % (errno, strerror)
except ValueError:
    print "Could not convert data to an integer."
except:
    print "Unexpected error:", sys.exc_info()[0]
    raise
```

The try ... except statement has an optional *else clause*, which, when present, must follow all except clauses. It is useful for code that must be executed if the try clause does not raise an exception. For example:

```
for arg in sys.argv[1:]:
    try:
        f = open(arg, 'r')
    except IOError:
        print 'cannot open', arg
    else:
        print arg, 'has', len(f.readlines()), 'lines'
        f.close()
```

The use of the else clause is better than adding additional code to the try clause because it avoids accidentally catching an exception that wasn't raised by the code being protected by the try ... except statement.

When an exception occurs, it may have an associated value, also known as the exception's *argument*. The presence and type of the argument depend on the exception type.

The except clause may specify a variable after the exception name (or tuple). The variable is bound to an exception instance with the arguments stored in instance.args. For convenience, the exception instance defines __getitem__ and __str__ so the arguments can be accessed or printed directly without having to reference .args.

But use of .args is discouraged. Instead, the preferred use is to pass a single argument to an exception (which can be a tuple if multiple arguments are needed) and have it bound to the message attribute. One my also instantiate an exception first before raising it and add any attributes to it as desired.

```
>>> try:
...     raise Exception('spam', 'eggs')
... except Exception, inst:
...     print type(inst)     # the exception instance
...     print inst.args      # arguments stored in .args
...     print inst           # __str__ allows args to
...                          # printed directly
...     x, y = inst          # __getitem__ allows args
...                          # to be unpacked directly
...     print 'x =', x
...     print 'y =', y
...
```

```
<type 'instance'>
('spam', 'eggs')
('spam', 'eggs')
x = spam
y = eggs
```

If an exception has an argument, it is printed as the last part ('detail') of the message for unhandled exceptions.

Exception handlers don't just handle exceptions if they occur immediately in the try clause, but also if they occur inside functions that are called (even indirectly) in the try clause. For example:

```
>>> def this_fails():
...     x = 1/0
...
>>> try:
...     this_fails()
... except ZeroDivisionError, detail:
...     print 'Handling run-time error:', detail
...
Handling run-time error: integer division or
 modulo by zero
```

8.4 Raising Exceptions

The raise statement allows the programmer to force a specified exception to occur. For example:

```
>>> raise NameError, 'HiThere'
Traceback (most recent call last):
  File "<stdin>", line 1, in ?
NameError: HiThere
```

The first argument to raise names the exception to be raised. The optional second argument specifies the exception's argument. Alternatively, the above could be written as raise NameError('HiThere'). Either form works fine, but there seems to be a growing stylistic preference for the latter.

If you need to determine whether an exception was raised but don't intend to handle it, a simpler form of the raise statement allows you to re-raise the exception:

```
>>> try:
...     raise NameError, 'HiThere'
... except NameError:
...     print 'An exception flew by!'
...     raise
...
An exception flew by!
Traceback (most recent call last):
  File "<stdin>", line 2, in ?
NameError: HiThere
```

8.5   User-defined Exceptions

Programs may name their own exceptions by creating a new exception class. Exceptions should typically be derived from the Exception class, either directly or indirectly. For example:

```
>>> class MyError(Exception):
...     def __init__(self, value):
...         self.value = value
...     def __str__(self):
...         return repr(self.value)
...
>>> try:
...     raise MyError(2*2)
... except MyError, e:
...     print 'My exception occurred, value:', e.value
...
My exception occurred, value: 4
>>> raise MyError, 'oops!'
Traceback (most recent call last):
  File "<stdin>", line 1, in ?
__main__.MyError: 'oops!'
```

In this example, the default __init__ of Exception has been overridden. The new behavior simply creates the *value* attribute. This replaces the default behavior of creating the *args* attribute.

Exception classes can be defined which do anything any other class can do, but are usually kept simple, often only offering a number of attributes that allow information about the error to be extracted by handlers for the exception. When creating a module that can raise several distinct errors, a common practice is to create a base class for exceptions defined by that module, and subclass that to create specific exception classes for different error conditions:

```
class Error(Exception):
    """Base class for exceptions in this module."""
    pass

class InputError(Error):
    """Exception raised for errors in the input.

    Attributes:
        expression -- input expression in which
                        the error occurred
        message -- explanation of the error
    """

    def __init__(self, expression, message):
        self.expression = expression
        self.message = message

class TransitionError(Error):
    """Raised when an operation attempts a state
    transition that's not allowed.

    Attributes:
        previous -- state at beginning of transition
        next -- attempted new state
        message -- explanation of why the specific
        transition is not allowed
    """

    def __init__(self, previous, next, message):
        self.previous = previous
        self.next = next
        self.message = message
```

Most exceptions are defined with names that end in "Error," similar to the naming of the standard exceptions.

Many standard modules define their own exceptions to report errors that may occur in functions they define. More information on classes is presented in chapter 9, "Classes."

8.6 Defining Clean-up Actions

The try statement has another optional clause which is intended to define clean-up actions that must be executed under all circumstances. For example:

```
>>> try:
...     raise KeyboardInterrupt
... finally:
...     print 'Goodbye, world!'
...
Goodbye, world!
Traceback (most recent call last):
  File "<stdin>", line 2, in ?
KeyboardInterrupt
```

A *finally clause* is always executed before leaving the try statement, whether an exception has occurred or not. When an exception has occurred in the try clause and has not been handled by an except clause (or it has occurred in a except or else clause), it is re-raised after the finally clause has been executed. The finally clause is also executed "on the way out" when any other clause of the try statement is left via a break, continue or return statement. A more complicated example:

```
>>> def divide(x, y):
...     try:
...         result = x / y
...     except ZeroDivisionError:
...         print "division by zero!"
...     else:
...         print "result is", result
...     finally:
...         print "executing finally clause"
...
>>> divide(2, 1)
result is 2
executing finally clause
>>> divide(2, 0)
division by zero!
executing finally clause
>>> divide("2", "1")
executing finally clause
Traceback (most recent call last):
  File "<stdin>", line 1, in ?
```

```
     File "<stdin>", line 3, in divide
TypeError: unsupported operand type(s) for /:
 'str' and 'str'
```

As you can see, the finally clause is executed in any event. The TypeError raised by dividing two strings is not handled by the except clause and therefore re-raised after the finally clauses has been executed.

In real world applications, the finally clause is useful for releasing external resources (such as files or network connections), regardless of whether the use of the resource was successful.

8.7 Predefined Clean-up Actions

Some objects define standard clean-up actions to be undertaken when the object is no longer needed, regardless of whether or not the operation using the object succeeded or failed. Look at the following example, which tries to open a file and print its contents to the screen.

```
for line in open("myfile.txt"):
    print line
```

The problem with this code is that it leaves the file open for an indeterminate amount of time after the code has finished executing. This is not an issue in simple scripts, but can be a problem for larger applications. The with statement allows objects like files to be used in a way that ensures they are always cleaned up promptly and correctly.

```
with open("myfile.txt") as f:
    for line in f:
        print line
```

After the statement is executed, the file f is always closed, even if a problem was encountered while processing the lines. Other objects which provide predefined clean-up actions will indicate this in their documentation.

9 Classes

Python's class mechanism adds classes to the language with a minimum of new syntax and semantics. It is a mixture of the class mechanisms found in C++ and Modula-3. As is true for modules, classes in Python do not put an absolute barrier between definition and user, but rather rely on the politeness of the user not to "break into the definition." The most important features of classes are retained with full power, however: the class inheritance mechanism allows multiple base classes, a derived class can override any methods of its base class or classes, and a method can call the method of a base class with the same name. Objects can contain an arbitrary amount of private data.

In C++ terminology, all class members (including the data members) are *public*, and all member functions are *virtual*. There are no special constructors or destructors. As in Modula-3, there are no shorthands for referencing the object's members from its methods: the method function is declared with an explicit first argument representing the object, which is provided implicitly by the call. As in Smalltalk, classes themselves are objects, albeit in the wider sense of the word: in Python, all data types are objects. This provides semantics for importing and renaming. Unlike C++ and Modula-3, built-in types can be used as base classes for extension by the user. Also, like in C++ but unlike in Modula-3, most built-in operators with special syntax (arithmetic operators, subscripting etc.) can be redefined for class instances.

9.1 A Word About Terminology

Lacking universally accepted terminology to talk about classes, I will make occasional use of Smalltalk and C++ terms. (I would use Modula-3 terms, since its object-oriented semantics are closer to those of Python than C++, but I expect that few readers have heard of it.)

Objects have individuality, and multiple names (in multiple scopes) can be bound to the same object. This is known as aliasing in other languages. This is usually not appreciated on a first glance at Python, and can be safely ignored when dealing with immutable basic types (numbers, strings, tuples). However, aliasing has an (intended!) effect on the semantics of Python code involving mutable objects such as lists, dictionaries, and most types representing entities outside the program (files, windows, etc.).

This is usually used to the benefit of the program, since aliases behave like pointers in some respects. For example, passing an object is cheap since only a pointer is passed by the implementation; and if a function modifies an object passed as an argument, the caller will see the change—this eliminates the need for two different argument passing mechanisms as in Pascal.

9.2 Python Scopes and Name Spaces

Before introducing classes, I first have to tell you something about Python's scope rules. Class definitions play some neat tricks with namespaces, and you need to know how scopes and namespaces work to fully understand what's going on. Incidentally, knowledge about this subject is useful for any advanced Python programmer.

Let's begin with some definitions.

A *namespace* is a mapping from names to objects. Most namespaces are currently implemented as Python dictionaries, but that's normally not noticeable in any way (except for performance), and it may change in the future. Examples of namespaces are: the set of built-in names (functions such as abs(), and built-in exception names); the global names in a module; and the local names in a function invocation. In a sense the set of attributes of an object also form a namespace. The important thing to know about namespaces is that there is absolutely no relation between names in different namespaces; for instance, two different modules may both define a function "maximize" without confusion—users of the modules must prefix it with the module name.

By the way, I use the word *attribute* for any name following a dot—for example, in the expression z.real, real is an attribute of the object z. Strictly speaking, references to names in modules are attribute references: in the expression modname.funcname, modname is a module object and funcname is an attribute of it. In this case there happens to be a straightforward mapping between the module's attributes and the global names defined in the module: they share the same namespace![1]

Attributes may be read-only or writable. In the latter case, assignment to attributes is possible. Module attributes are writable: you can write assignments such as 'modname.the_answer = 42'. Writable attributes may

---

[1]Except for one thing. Module objects have a secret read-only attribute called __dict__ which returns the dictionary used to implement the module's namespace; the name __dict__ is an attribute but not a global name. Obviously, using this violates the abstraction of namespace implementation, and should be restricted to things like post-mortem debuggers.

also be deleted with the del statement. For example, 'del modname.the_ answer' will remove the attribute the_answer from the object named by modname.

Name spaces are created at different moments and have different lifetimes. The namespace containing the built-in names is created when the Python interpreter starts up, and is never deleted. The global namespace for a module is created when the module definition is read in; normally, module namespaces also last until the interpreter quits. The statements executed by the top-level invocation of the interpreter, either read from a script file or interactively, are considered part of a module called __main__, so they have their own global namespace. (The built-in names actually also live in a module; this is called __builtin__.)

The local namespace for a function is created when the function is called, and deleted when the function returns or raises an exception that is not handled within the function. (Actually, forgetting would be a better way to describe what actually happens.) Of course, recursive invocations each have their own local namespace.

A *scope* is a textual region of a Python program where a namespace is directly accessible. "Directly accessible" here means that an unqualified reference to a name attempts to find the name in the namespace.

Although scopes are determined statically, they are used dynamically. At any time during execution, there are at least three nested scopes whose namespaces are directly accessible: the innermost scope, which is searched first, contains the local names; the namespaces of any enclosing functions, which are searched starting with the nearest enclosing scope; the middle scope, searched next, contains the current module's global names; and the outermost scope (searched last) is the namespace containing built-in names.

If a name is declared global, then all references and assignments go directly to the middle scope containing the module's global names. Otherwise, all variables found outside of the innermost scope are read-only (an attempt to write to such a variable will simply create a *new* local variable in the innermost scope, leaving the identically named outer variable unchanged).

Usually, the local scope references the local names of the (textually) current function. Outside functions, the local scope references the same namespace as the global scope: the module's namespace. Class definitions place yet another namespace in the local scope.

It is important to realize that scopes are determined textually: the global scope of a function defined in a module is that module's namespace, no matter from where or by what alias the function is called. On the other hand, the actual search for names is done dynamically, at run time—however, the language definition is evolving towards static name resolution, at "compile" time, so don't rely on dynamic name resolution! (In fact, local variables are already determined statically.)

A special quirk of Python is that assignments always go into the innermost scope. Assignments do not copy data—they just bind names to objects. The same is true for deletions: the statement 'del x' removes the binding of x from the namespace referenced by the local scope. In fact, all operations that introduce new names use the local scope: in particular, import statements and function definitions bind the module or function name in the local scope. (The global statement can be used to indicate that particular variables live in the global scope.)

9.3   A First Look at Classes

Classes introduce a little bit of new syntax, three new object types, and some new semantics.

9.3.1   Class Definition Syntax

The simplest form of class definition looks like this:

```
class ClassName:
    <statement-1>
    .
    .
    .
    <statement-N>
```

Class definitions, like function definitions (def statements) must be executed before they have any effect. (You could conceivably place a class definition in a branch of an if statement, or inside a function.)

In practice, the statements inside a class definition will usually be function definitions, but other statements are allowed, and sometimes useful—we'll come back to this later. The function definitions inside a class normally have a peculiar form of argument list, dictated by the calling conventions for methods—again, this is explained later.

When a class definition is entered, a new namespace is created, and used as the local scope—thus, all assignments to local variables go into this new namespace. In particular, function definitions bind the name of the new function here.

When a class definition is left normally (via the end), a *class object* is created. This is basically a wrapper around the contents of the namespace created by the class definition; we'll learn more about class objects in the next section. The original local scope (the one in effect just before the class definition was entered) is reinstated, and the class object is bound here to the class name given in the class definition header (ClassName in the example).

9.3.2 Class Objects

Class objects support two kinds of operations: *attribute references* and *instantiation*.

Attribute references use the standard syntax used for all attribute references in Python: obj.name. Valid attribute names are all the names that were in the class's namespace when the class object was created. So, if the class definition looked like this:

```
class MyClass:
    "A simple example class"
    i = 12345
    def f(self):
        return 'hello world'
```

then MyClass.i and MyClass.f are valid attribute references, returning an integer and a function object, respectively. Class attributes can also be assigned to, so you can change the value of MyClass.i by assignment. __doc__ is also a valid attribute, returning the docstring belonging to the class: "A simple example class".

Class *instantiation* uses function notation. Just pretend that the class object is a parameterless function that returns a new instance of the class. For example (assuming the above class):

```
x = MyClass()
```

creates a new *instance* of the class and assigns this object to the local variable x.

The instantiation operation ("calling" a class object) creates an empty object. Many classes like to create objects with instances customized to a specific initial state. Therefore a class may define a special method named __init__(), like this:

```
def __init__(self):
    self.data = []
```

When a class defines an __init__() method, class instantiation automatically invokes __init__() for the newly-created class instance. So in this example, a new, initialized instance can be obtained by:

```
x = MyClass()
```

Of course, the __init__() method may have arguments for greater flexibility. In that case, arguments given to the class instantiation operator are passed on to __init__(). For example,

```
>>> class Complex:
...     def __init__(self, realpart, imagpart):
...         self.r = realpart
...         self.i = imagpart
...
>>> x = Complex(3.0, -4.5)
>>> x.r, x.i
(3.0, -4.5)
```

9.3.3   Instance Objects

Now what can we do with instance objects? The only operations understood by instance objects are attribute references. There are two kinds of valid attribute names, data attributes and methods.

Data attributes correspond to "instance variables" in Smalltalk, and to "data members" in C++. Data attributes need not be declared; like local variables, they spring into existence when they are first assigned to. For example, if x is the instance of MyClass created above, the following piece of code will print the value 16, without leaving a trace:

```
x.counter = 1
while x.counter < 10:
    x.counter = x.counter * 2
print x.counter
del x.counter
```

The other kind of instance attribute reference is a *method*. A method is a function that "belongs to" an object. (In Python, the term method is not unique to class instances: other object types can have methods as well. For example, list objects have methods called append, insert, remove, sort, and so on. However, in the following discussion, we'll use the term method exclusively to mean methods of class instance objects, unless explicitly stated otherwise.)

Valid method names of an instance object depend on its class. By definition, all attributes of a class that are function objects define corresponding methods of its instances. So in our example, x.f is a valid method reference, since MyClass.f is a function, but x.i is not, since MyClass.i is not. But x.f is not the same thing as MyClass.f—it is a *method object*, not a function object.

9.3.4   Method Objects

Usually, a method is called right after it is bound:

```
x.f()
```

In the MyClass example, this will return the string 'hello world'. However, it is not necessary to call a method right away: x.f is a method object, and can be stored away and called at a later time. For example:

```
xf = x.f
while True:
    print xf()
```

will continue to print 'hello world' until the end of time.

What exactly happens when a method is called? You may have noticed that x.f() was called without an argument above, even though the function definition for f specified an argument. What happened to the argument? Surely Python raises an exception when a function that requires an argument is called without any—even if the argument isn't actually used ...

Actually, you may have guessed the answer: the special thing about methods is that the object is passed as the first argument of the function. In our example, the call x.f() is exactly equivalent to MyClass.f(x). In general, calling a method with a list of n arguments is equivalent to calling the corresponding function with an argument list that is created by inserting the method's object before the first argument.

If you still don't understand how methods work, a look at the implementation can perhaps clarify matters. When an instance attribute is referenced that isn't a data attribute, its class is searched. If the name denotes a valid class attribute that is a function object, a method object is created by packing (pointers to) the instance object and the function object just found together in an abstract object: this is the method object. When the method object is called with an argument list, it is unpacked again, a new argument list is constructed from the instance object and the original argument list, and the function object is called with this new argument list.

9.4 Random Remarks

Data attributes override method attributes with the same name; to avoid accidental name conflicts, which may cause hard-to-find bugs in large programs, it is wise to use some kind of convention that minimizes the chance of conflicts. Possible conventions include capitalizing method names, prefixing data attribute names with a small unique string (perhaps just an underscore), or using verbs for methods and nouns for data attributes.

Data attributes may be referenced by methods as well as by ordinary users ("clients") of an object. In other words, classes are not usable to implement pure abstract data types. In fact, nothing in Python makes it possible to enforce data hiding—it is all based upon convention. (On the other hand, the Python implementation, written in C, can completely hide implementation details and control access to an object if necessary; this can be used by extensions to Python written in C.)

Clients should use data attributes with care—clients may mess up invariants maintained by the methods by stamping on their data attributes. Note that clients may add data attributes of their own to an instance object without affecting the validity of the methods, as long as name conflicts are avoided—again, a naming convention can save a lot of headaches here.

There is no shorthand for referencing data attributes (or other methods!) from within methods. I find that this actually increases the readability of methods: there is no chance of confusing local variables and instance variables when glancing through a method.

Often, the first argument of a method is called self. This is nothing more than a convention: the name self has absolutely no special meaning to Python. (Note, however, that by not following the convention your code may be less readable to other Python programmers, and it is also conceivable that a *class browser* program might be written that relies upon such a convention.)

Any function object that is a class attribute defines a method for instances of that class. It is not necessary that the function definition is textually enclosed in the class definition: assigning a function object to a local variable in the class is also ok. For example:

```
# Function defined outside the class
def f1(self, x, y):
```

```
        return min(x, x+y)

    class C:
        f = f1
        def g(self):
            return 'hello world'
        h = g
```

Now f, g and h are all attributes of class C that refer to function objects, and consequently they are all methods of instances of C—h being exactly equivalent to g. Note that this practice usually only serves to confuse the reader of a program.

Methods may call other methods by using method attributes of the self argument:

```
    class Bag:
        def __init__(self):
            self.data = []
        def add(self, x):
            self.data.append(x)
        def addtwice(self, x):
            self.add(x)
            self.add(x)
```

Methods may reference global names in the same way as ordinary functions. The global scope associated with a method is the module containing the class definition. (The class itself is never used as a global scope!) While one rarely encounters a good reason for using global data in a method, there are many legitimate uses of the global scope: for one thing, functions and modules imported into the global scope can be used by methods, as well as functions and classes defined in it. Usually, the class containing the method is itself defined in this global scope, and in the next section we'll find some good reasons why a method would want to reference its own class!

9.5   Inheritance

Of course, a language feature would not be worthy of the name "class" without supporting inheritance. The syntax for a derived class definition looks like this:

```
    class DerivedClassName(BaseClassName):
```

```
<statement-1>
       .
       .
       .
<statement-N>
```

The name BaseClassName must be defined in a scope containing the derived class definition. In place of a base class name, other arbitrary expressions are also allowed. This can be useful, for example, when the base class is defined in another module:

```
class DerivedClassName(modname.BaseClassName):
```

Execution of a derived class definition proceeds the same as for a base class. When the class object is constructed, the base class is remembered. This is used for resolving attribute references: if a requested attribute is not found in the class, the search proceeds to look in the base class. This rule is applied recursively if the base class itself is derived from some other class.

There's nothing special about instantiation of derived classes: DerivedClassName() creates a new instance of the class. Method references are resolved as follows: the corresponding class attribute is searched, descending down the chain of base classes if necessary, and the method reference is valid if this yields a function object.

Derived classes may override methods of their base classes. Because methods have no special privileges when calling other methods of the same object, a method of a base class that calls another method defined in the same base class may end up calling a method of a derived class that overrides it. (For C++ programmers: all methods in Python are effectively virtual.)

An overriding method in a derived class may in fact want to extend rather than simply replace the base class method of the same name. There is a simple way to call the base class method directly: just call 'BaseClassName.methodname(self, arguments)'. This is occasionally useful to clients as well. (Note that this only works if the base class is defined or imported directly in the global scope.)

9.5.1 Multiple Inheritance

Python supports a limited form of multiple inheritance as well. A class definition with multiple base classes looks like this:

```
class DerivedClassName(Base1, Base2, Base3):
```

```
<statement-1>
  .
  .
  .
<statement-N>
```

The only rule necessary to explain the semantics is the resolution rule used for class attribute references. This is depth-first, left-to-right. Thus, if an attribute is not found in `DerivedClassName`, it is searched in `Base1`, then (recursively) in the base classes of `Base1`, and only if it is not found there, it is searched in `Base2`, and so on.

(To some people breadth first—searching `Base2` and `Base3` before the base classes of `Base1`—looks more natural. However, this would require you to know whether a particular attribute of `Base1` is actually defined in `Base1` or in one of its base classes before you can figure out the consequences of a name conflict with an attribute of `Base2`. The depth-first rule makes no differences between direct and inherited attributes of `Base1`.)

It is clear that indiscriminate use of multiple inheritance is a maintenance nightmare, given the reliance in Python on conventions to avoid accidental name conflicts. A well-known problem with multiple inheritance is a class derived from two classes that happen to have a common base class. While it is easy enough to figure out what happens in this case (the instance will have a single copy of "instance variables" or data attributes used by the common base class), it is not clear that these semantics are in any way useful.

9.6 Private Variables

There is limited support for class-private identifiers. Any identifier of the form `__spam` (at least two leading underscores, at most one trailing underscore) is textually replaced with `_classname__spam`, where `classname` is the current class name with leading underscore(s) stripped. This mangling is done without regard to the syntactic position of the identifier, so it can be used to define class-private instance and class variables, methods, variables stored in globals, and even variables stored in instances. private to this class on instances of *other* classes. Truncation may occur when the mangled name would be longer than 255 characters. Outside classes, or when the class name consists of only underscores, no mangling occurs.

Name mangling is intended to give classes an easy way to define "private" instance variables and methods, without having to worry about instance variables defined by derived classes, or mucking with instance variables by code outside the class. Note that the mangling rules are designed mostly to avoid accidents; it still is possible for a determined soul to access or modify a variable that is considered private. This can even be useful in special circumstances, such as in the debugger, and that's one reason why this loophole is not closed. (Buglet: derivation of a class with the same name as the base class makes use of private variables of the base class possible.)

Notice that code passed to exec, eval() or execfile() does not consider the classname of the invoking class to be the current class; this is similar to the effect of the global statement, the effect of which is likewise restricted to code that is byte-compiled together. The same restriction applies to getattr(), setattr() and delattr(), as well as when referencing __ dict__ directly.

9.7   Odds and Ends

Sometimes it is useful to have a data type similar to the Pascal "record" or C "struct", bundling together a few named data items. An empty class definition will do nicely:

```
class Employee:
    pass

john = Employee() # Create an empty employee record

# Fill the fields of the record
john.name = 'John Doe'
john.dept = 'computer lab'
john.salary = 1000
```

A piece of Python code that expects a particular abstract data type can often be passed a class that emulates the methods of that data type instead. For instance, if you have a function that formats some data from a file object, you can define a class with methods read() and readline() that get the data from a string buffer instead, and pass it as an argument.

Instance method objects have attributes, too: m.im_self is the instance object with the method m, and m.im_func is the function object corresponding to the method.

9.8   Exceptions Are Classes Too

User-defined exceptions are identified by classes as well. Using this mechanism it is possible to create extensible hierarchies of exceptions.

There are two valid (semantic) forms for the raise statement:

```
raise Class, instance
```

```
raise instance
```

In the first form, instance must be an instance of Class or of a class derived from it. The second form is a shorthand for:

```
raise instance.__class__, instance
```

A class in an except clause is compatible with an exception if it is the same class or a base class thereof (but not the other way around—an except clause listing a derived class is not compatible with a base class). For example, the following code will print B, C, D in that order:

```
class B:
    pass
class C(B):
    pass
class D(C):
    pass

for c in [B, C, D]:
    try:
        raise c()
    except D:
        print "D"
    except C:
        print "C"
    except B:
        print "B"
```

Note that if the except clauses were reversed (with 'except B' first), it would have printed B, B, B—the first matching except clause is triggered.

When an error message is printed for an unhandled exception, the exception's class name is printed, then a colon and a space, and finally the instance converted to a string using the built-in function str().

9.9 Iterators

By now you have probably noticed that most container objects can be looped over using a for statement:

```
for element in [1, 2, 3]:
    print element
for element in (1, 2, 3):
    print element
for key in {'one':1, 'two':2}:
    print key
for char in "123":
    print char
for line in open("myfile.txt"):
    print line
```

This style of access is clear, concise, and convenient. The use of iterators pervades and unifies Python. Behind the scenes, the for statement
calls iter() on the container object. The function returns an iterator
object that defines the method next() which accesses elements in the
container one at a time. When there are no more elements, next() raises
a StopIteration exception which tells the for loop to terminate. This
example shows how it all works:

```
>>> s = 'abc'
>>> it = iter(s)
>>> it
<iterator object at 0x00A1DB50>
>>> it.next()
'a'
>>> it.next()
'b'
>>> it.next()
'c'
>>> it.next()

Traceback (most recent call last):
  File "<stdin>", line 1, in ?
    it.next()
StopIteration
```

Having seen the mechanics behind the iterator protocol, it is easy to add
iterator behavior to your classes. Define a __iter__() method which
returns an object with a next() method. If the class defines next(),
then __iter__() can just return self:

```
class Reverse:
    "Iterator for looping over a sequence backwards"
```

```
    def __init__(self, data):
        self.data = data
        self.index = len(data)
    def __iter__(self):
        return self
    def next(self):
        if self.index == 0:
            raise StopIteration
        self.index = self.index - 1
        return self.data[self.index]

>>> for char in Reverse('spam'):
...     print char
...
m
a
p
s
```

9.10   Generators

Generators are a simple and powerful tool for creating iterators. They are written like regular functions but use the yield statement whenever they want to return data. Each time next() is called, the generator resumes where it left-off (it remembers all the data values and which statement was last executed). An example shows that generators can be trivially easy to create:

```
def reverse(data):
    for index in range(len(data)-1, -1, -1):
        yield data[index]

>>> for char in reverse('golf'):
...     print char
...
f
l
o
g
```

Anything that can be done with generators can also be done with class based iterators as described in the previous section. What makes generators so compact is that the __iter__() and next() methods are created automatically.

Another key feature is that the local variables and execution state are automatically saved between calls. This made the function easier to write and much more clear than an approach using instance variables like self. index and self.data.

In addition to automatic method creation and saving program state, when generators terminate, they automatically raise StopIteration. In combination, these features make it easy to create iterators with no more effort than writing a regular function.

9.11 Generator Expressions

Some simple generators can be coded succinctly as expressions using a syntax similar to list comprehensions but with parentheses instead of square brackets. These expressions are designed for situations where the generator is used right away by an enclosing function. Generator expressions are more compact but less versatile than full generator definitions and tend to be more memory friendly than equivalent list comprehensions.

Examples:

```
>>> sum(i*i for i in range(10))      # sum of squares
285

>>> xvec = [10, 20, 30]
>>> yvec = [7, 5, 3]
>>> sum(x*y for x,y in zip(xvec, yvec)) # dot product
260

>>> from math import pi, sin
>>> sine_table = dict((x, sin(x*pi/180)) for x in
 range(0, 91))

>>> unique_words = set(word  for line in page  for word
 in line.split())

>>> valedictorian = max((student.gpa, student.name) for
 student in graduates)

>>> data = 'golf'
>>> list(data[i] for i in range(len(data)-1,-1,-1))
['f', 'l', 'o', 'g']
```

10 Brief Tour of the Standard Library

10.1 Operating System Interface

The os module provides dozens of functions for interacting with the operating system:

```
>>> import os
>>> os.system('time 0:02')
0
>>> os.getcwd() # Return the current working directory
'C:\\Python25'
>>> os.chdir('/server/accesslogs')
```

Be sure to use the 'import os' style instead of 'from os import *'. This will keep os.open() from shadowing the builtin open() function which operates much differently.

The builtin dir() and help() functions are useful as interactive aids for working with large modules like os:

```
>>> import os
>>> dir(os)
<returns a list of all module functions>
>>> help(os)
<returns an extensive manual page created from the
 module's docstrings>
```

For daily file and directory management tasks, the shutil module provides a higher level interface that is easier to use:

```
>>> import shutil
>>> shutil.copyfile('data.db', 'archive.db')
>>> shutil.move('/build/executables', 'installdir')
```

10.2 File Wildcards

The glob module provides a function for making file lists from directory wildcard searches:

```
>>> import glob
>>> glob.glob('*.py')
['primes.py', 'random.py', 'quote.py']
```

10.3 Command Line Arguments

Common utility scripts often need to process command line arguments. These arguments are stored in the sys module's *argv* attribute as a list. For instance the following output results from running 'python demo.py one two three' at the command line:

```
>>> import sys
>>> print sys.argv
['demo.py', 'one', 'two', 'three']
```

The getopt module processes *sys.argv* using the conventions of the UNIX getopt() function. More powerful and flexible command line processing is provided by the optparse module.

10.4 Error Output Redirection and Program Termination

The sys module also has attributes for *stdin*, *stdout*, and *stderr*. The latter is useful for emitting warnings and error messages to make them visible even when *stdout* has been redirected:

```
>>> sys.stderr.write('Warning, log file not found\n')
Warning, log file not found
```

The most direct way to terminate a script is to use 'sys.exit()'.

10.5 String Pattern Matching

The re module provides regular expression tools for advanced string processing. For complex matching and manipulation, regular expressions offer succinct, optimized solutions:

```
>>> import re
>>> re.findall(r'\bf[a-z]*', 'which foot or hand fell')
['foot', 'fell']
>>> re.sub(r'(\b[a-z]+) \1', r'\1', 'cat in the the hat')
'cat in the hat'
```

When only simple capabilities are needed, string methods are preferred because they are easier to read and debug:

```
>>> 'tea for too'.replace('too', 'two')
'tea for two'
```

10.6   Mathematics

The math module gives access to the underlying C library functions for floating point math:

```
>>> import math
>>> math.cos(math.pi / 4.0)
0.70710678118654757
>>> math.log(1024, 2)
10.0
```

The random module provides tools for making random selections:

```
>>> import random
>>> random.choice(['apple', 'pear', 'banana'])
'apple'
>>> random.sample(xrange(100), 10)    # sampling without
                                      # replacement
[30, 83, 16, 4, 8, 81, 41, 50, 18, 33]
>>> random.random()     # random float
0.17970987693706186
>>> random.randrange(6) # sample from [0,1,2,3,4,5]
4
```

10.7   Internet Access

There are a number of modules for accessing the internet and processing internet protocols. Two of the simplest are urllib2 for retrieving data from urls and smtplib for sending mail:

```
>>> import urllib2
>>> url = 'http://tycho.usno.navy.mil/cgi-bin/timer.pl'
>>> for line in urllib2.urlopen(url):
...     if 'EST' in line or 'EDT' in line:
...         print line

<BR>Nov. 25, 09:43:32 PM EST

>>> import smtplib
>>> server = smtplib.SMTP('localhost')
>>> server.sendmail('soothsayer@example.org',
                    'jcaesar@example.org',
"""To: jcaesar@example.org
From: soothsayer@example.org

Beware the Ides of March.
""")
>>> server.quit()
```

10.8   Dates and Times

The datetime module supplies classes for manipulating dates and times in both simple and complex ways. While date and time arithmetic is supported, the focus of the implementation is on efficient member extraction for output formatting and manipulation. The module also supports objects that are timezone aware.

```
# dates are easily constructed and formatted
>>> from datetime import date
>>> now = date.today()
>>> now
datetime.date(2003, 12, 2)
>>> now.strftime("%m-%d-%y. %d %b %Y is a %A on the %d
 day of %B.")
'12-02-03. 02 Dec 2003 is a Tuesday on the 02 day of
 December.'

# dates support calendar arithmetic
>>> birthday = date(1964, 7, 31)
>>> age = now - birthday
>>> age.days
14368
```

10.9   Data Compression

Common data archiving and compression formats are directly supported
by modules including: zlib, gzip, bz2, zipfile, and tarfile.

```
>>> import zlib
>>> s = 'witch which has which witches wrist watch'
>>> len(s)
41
>>> t = zlib.compress(s)
>>> len(t)
37
>>> zlib.decompress(t)
'witch which has which witches wrist watch'
>>> zlib.crc32(s)
226805979
```

10.10   Performance Measurement

Some Python users develop a deep interest in knowing the relative performance of different approaches to the same problem. Python provides
a measurement tool that answers those questions immediately.

For example, it may be tempting to use the tuple packing and unpacking
feature instead of the traditional approach to swapping arguments. The
timeit module quickly demonstrates a modest performance advantage:

```
>>> from timeit import Timer
>>> Timer('t=a; a=b; b=t', 'a=1; b=2').timeit()
0.57535828626024577
>>> Timer('a,b = b,a', 'a=1; b=2').timeit()
0.54962537085770791
```

In contrast to timeit's fine level of granularity, the profile and pstats
modules provide tools for identifying time critical sections in larger blocks
of code.

10.11   Quality Control

One approach for developing high quality software is to write tests for
each function as it is developed and to run those tests frequently during
the development process.

The doctest module provides a tool for scanning a module and validating tests embedded in a program's docstrings. Test construction is as simple as cutting-and-pasting a typical call along with its results into the docstring. This improves the documentation by providing the user with an example and it allows the doctest module to make sure the code remains true to the documentation:

```
def average(values):
    """Computes the arithmetic mean of a list of numbers.

    >>> print average([20, 30, 70])
    40.0
    """
    return sum(values, 0.0) / len(values)

import doctest
doctest.testmod()   # automatically validate the tests
```

The unittest module is not as effortless as the doctest module, but it allows a more comprehensive set of tests to be maintained in a separate file:

```
import unittest

class TestStatisticalFunctions(unittest.TestCase):

    def test_average(self):
        self.assertEqual(average([20, 30, 70]), 40.0)
        self.assertEqual(round(average([1, 5, 7]), 1), 4.3)
        self.assertRaises(ZeroDivisionError, average, [])
        self.assertRaises(TypeError, average, 20, 30, 70)

unittest.main() # Calling from the command line invokes
                # all tests
```

10.12 Batteries Included

Python has a "batteries included" philosophy. This is best seen through the sophisticated and robust capabilities of its larger packages. For example:

- The xmlrpclib and SimpleXMLRPCServer modules make implementing remote procedure calls into an almost trivial task. Despite the modules names, no direct knowledge or handling of XML is needed.

- The email package is a library for managing email messages, including MIME and other RFC 2822-based message documents. Unlike smtplib and poplib which actually send and receive messages, the email package has a complete toolset for building or decoding complex message structures (including attachments) and for implementing internet encoding and header protocols.

- The xml.dom and xml.sax packages provide robust support for parsing this popular data interchange format. Likewise, the csv module supports direct reads and writes in a common database format. Together, these modules and packages greatly simplify data interchange between python applications and other tools.

- Internationalization is supported by a number of modules including gettext, locale, and the codecs package.

11 Brief Tour of the Standard Library – Part II

This second tour covers more advanced modules that support professional programming needs. These modules rarely occur in small scripts.

11.1 Output Formatting

The repr module provides a version of repr() customized for abbreviated displays of large or deeply nested containers:

```
>>> import repr
>>> repr.repr(set('supercalifragilisticexpialidocious'))
"set(['a', 'c', 'd', 'e', 'f', 'g', ...])"
```

The pprint module offers more sophisticated control over printing both built-in and user defined objects in a way that is readable by the interpreter. When the result is longer than one line, the "pretty printer" adds line breaks and indentation to more clearly reveal data structure:

```
>>> import pprint
>>> t = [[[['black', 'cyan'], 'white', ['green', 'red']],
 [['magenta', 'yellow'], 'blue']]]
>>> pprint.pprint(t, width=30)
[[[['black', 'cyan'],
    'white',
    ['green', 'red']],
  [['magenta', 'yellow'],
    'blue']]]
```

The textwrap module formats paragraphs of text to fit a given screen width:

```
>>> import textwrap
>>> doc = """The wrap() method is just like
... fill() except that it returns a list of
... strings instead of one big string with
... newlines to separate the wrapped
```

```
... lines."""
...
>>> print textwrap.fill(doc, width=40)
The wrap() method is just like fill()
except that it returns a list of strings
instead of one big string with newlines
to separate the wrapped lines.
```

The locale module accesses a database of culture specific data formats. The grouping attribute of locale's format function provides a direct way of formatting numbers with group separators:

```
>>> import locale
>>> locale.setlocale(locale.LC_ALL,
                     'English_United States.1252')
'English_United States.1252'
>>> conv = locale.localeconv()  # get map of conventions
>>> x = 1234567.8
>>> locale.format("%d", x, grouping=True)
'1,234,567'
>>> locale.format("%s%.*f", (conv['currency_symbol'],
...         conv['frac_digits'], x), grouping=True)
'$1,234,567.80'
```

11.2 Templating

The string module includes a versatile Template class with a simplified syntax suitable for editing by end-users. This allows users to customize their applications without having to alter the application.

The format uses placeholder names formed by '$' with valid Python identifiers (alphanumeric characters and underscores). Surrounding the placeholder with braces allows it to be followed by more alphanumeric letters with no intervening spaces. Writing '$$' creates a single escaped '$':

```
>>> from string import Template
>>> t = Template('${village}folk send $$10 to $cause.')
>>> t.substitute(village='Nottingham', cause='the ditch
 fund')
'Nottinghamfolk send $10 to the ditch fund.'
```

The substitute method raises a KeyError when a placeholder is not supplied in a dictionary or a keyword argument. For mail-merge style applications, user supplied data may be incomplete and the safe_substitute

method may be more appropriate—it will leave placeholders unchanged
if data is missing:

```
>>> t = Template('Return the $item to $owner.')
>>> d = dict(item='unladen swallow')
>>> t.substitute(d)
Traceback (most recent call last):
  . . .
KeyError: 'owner'
>>> t.safe_substitute(d)
'Return the unladen swallow to $owner.'
```

Template subclasses can specify a custom delimiter. For example, a batch
renaming utility for a photo browser may elect to use percent signs for
placeholders such as the current date, image sequence number, or file
format:

```
>>> import time, os.path
>>> photofiles = ['K74.jpg', 'K76.jpg', 'K77.jpg']
>>> class BatchRename(Template):
...     delimiter = '%'
>>> fmt = raw_input('Rename as (%d-date %n-no %f-fmt): ')
Rename as (%d-date %n-no %f-fmt): Pic_%n%f

>>> t = BatchRename(fmt)
>>> date = time.strftime('%d%b%y')
>>> for i, filename in enumerate(photofiles):
...     base, ext = os.path.splitext(filename)
...     newname = t.substitute(d=date, n=i, f=ext)
...     print '%s --> %s' % (filename, newname)

K74.jpg --> Pic_0.jpg
K76.jpg --> Pic_1.jpg
K77.jpg --> Pic_2.jpg
```

Another application for templating is separating program logic from the
details of multiple output formats. This makes it possible to substitute
custom templates for XML files, plain text reports, and HTML web reports.

11.3 Working with Binary Data Record Layouts

The struct module provides pack() and unpack() functions for working with variable length binary record formats. The following example shows how to loop through header information in a ZIP file (with pack codes "H" and "L" representing two and four byte unsigned numbers respectively):

```
import struct

data = open('myfile.zip', 'rb').read()
start = 0
for i in range(3): # show the first 3 file headers
    start += 14
    fields = struct.unpack('LLLHH', data[start:start+16])
    crc32, comp, uncomp, filenamesize, extra = fields

    start += 16
    filename = data[start:start+filenamesize]
    start += filenamesize
    extra = data[start:start+extra]
    print filename, hex(crc32), comp, uncomp

    start += extra + comp    # skip to the next header
```

11.4 Multi-threading

Threading is a technique for decoupling tasks which are not sequentially dependent. Threads can be used to improve the responsiveness of applications that accept user input while other tasks run in the background. A related use case is running I/O in parallel with computations in another thread.

The following code shows how the high level threading module can run tasks in background while the main program continues to run:

```
import threading, zipfile

class AsyncZip(threading.Thread):
    def __init__(self, infile, outfile):
        threading.Thread.__init__(self)
        self.infile = infile
        self.outfile = outfile
```

```
def run(self):
    f = zipfile.ZipFile(self.outfile, 'w',
                        zipfile.ZIP_DEFLATED)
    f.write(self.infile)
    f.close()
    print 'Finished background zip of: ', self.infile

background = AsyncZip('mydata.txt', 'myarchive.zip')
background.start()
print 'The main program continues to run in foreground.'

background.join()    # Wait for background task to finish
print 'Main program waited until background was done.'
```

The principal challenge of multi-threaded applications is coordinating threads that share data or other resources. To that end, the threading module provides a number of synchronization primitives including locks, events, condition variables, and semaphores.

While those tools are powerful, minor design errors can result in problems that are difficult to reproduce. So, the preferred approach to task coordination is to concentrate all access to a resource in a single thread and then use the Queue module to feed that thread with requests from other threads. Applications using Queue objects for inter-thread communication and coordination are easier to design, more readable, and more reliable.

11.5 Logging

The logging module offers a full featured and flexible logging system. At its simplest, log messages are sent to a file or to sys.stderr:

```
import logging
logging.debug('Debugging information')
logging.info('Informational message')
logging.warning('Warning:file %s not found', 'run.rc')
logging.error('Error occurred')
logging.critical('Critical error -- shutting down')
```

This produces the following output:

```
WARNING:root:Warning:file run.rc not found
ERROR:root:Error occurred
CRITICAL:root:Critical error -- shutting down
```

By default, informational and debugging messages are suppressed and the output is sent to standard error. Other output options include routing messages through email, datagrams, sockets, or to an HTTP Server. New filters can select different routing based on message priority: DEBUG, INFO, WARNING, ERROR, and CRITICAL.

The logging system can be configured directly from Python or can be loaded from a user editable configuration file for customized logging without altering the application.

11.6 Weak References

Python does automatic memory management (reference counting for most objects and garbage collection to eliminate cycles). The memory is freed shortly after the last reference to it has been eliminated.

This approach works fine for most applications but occasionally there is a need to track objects only as long as they are being used by something else. Unfortunately, just tracking them creates a reference that makes them permanent. The weakref module provides tools for tracking objects without creating a reference. When the object is no longer needed, it is automatically removed from a weakref table and a callback is triggered for weakref objects. Typical applications include caching objects that are expensive to create:

```
>>> import weakref, gc
>>> class A:
...     def __init__(self, value):
...             self.value = value
...     def __repr__(self):
...             return str(self.value)
...
>>> a = A(10)     # create a reference
>>> d = weakref.WeakValueDictionary()
>>> d['primary'] = a # does not create a reference
>>> d['primary'] # fetch the object if it is still alive
10
>>> del a        # remove the one reference
>>> gc.collect() # run garbage collection right away
0
>>> d['primary'] # entry was automatically removed
Traceback (most recent call last):
  File "<pyshell#108>", line 1, in -toplevel-
    d['primary'] # entry was automatically removed
```

```
  File "C:/PY24/lib/weakref.py", line 46, in __getitem__
    o = self.data[key]()
KeyError: 'primary'
```

11.7   Tools for Working with Lists

Many data structure needs can be met with the built-in list type. However, sometimes there is a need for alternative implementations with different performance trade-offs.

The array module provides an array() object that is like a list that stores only homogenous data and stores it more compactly. The following example shows an array of numbers stored as two byte unsigned binary numbers (typecode "H") rather than the usual 16 bytes per entry for regular lists of python int objects:

```
>>> from array import array
>>> a = array('H', [4000, 10, 700, 22222])
>>> sum(a)
26932
>>> a[1:3]
array('H', [10, 700])
```

The collections module provides a deque() object that is like a list with faster appends and pops from the left side but slower lookups in the middle. These objects are well suited for implementing queues and breadth first tree searches:

```
>>> from collections import deque
>>> d = deque(["task1", "task2", "task3"])
>>> d.append("task4")
>>> print "Handling", d.popleft()
Handling task1
```

The code for a breadth first search looks like this:

```
unsearched = deque([starting_node])
def breadth_first_search(unsearched):
    node = unsearched.popleft()
    for m in gen_moves(node):
        if is_goal(m):
            return m
        unsearched.append(m)
```

In addition to alternative list implementations, the library also offers other tools such as the `bisect` module with functions for manipulating sorted lists:

```
>>> import bisect
>>> scores = [(100, 'perl'), (200, 'tcl'), (400, 'lua'),
              (500, 'python')]
>>> bisect.insort(scores, (300, 'ruby'))
>>> scores
[(100, 'perl'), (200, 'tcl'), (300, 'ruby'),
 (400, 'lua'), (500, 'python')]
```

The `heapq` module provides functions for implementing heaps based on regular lists. The lowest valued entry is always kept at position zero. This is useful for applications which repeatedly access the smallest element but do not want to run a full list sort:

```
>>> from heapq import heapify, heappop, heappush
>>> data = [1, 3, 5, 7, 9, 2, 4, 6, 8, 0]
>>> heapify(data) # rearrange the list into heap order
>>> heappush(data, -5)          # add a new entry
>>> [heappop(data) for i in range(3)]  # fetch the three
                                       # smallest entries
[-5, 0, 1]
```

11.8 Decimal Floating Point Arithmetic

The `decimal` module offers a `Decimal` datatype for decimal floating point arithmetic. Compared to the built-in `float` implementation of binary floating point, the new class is especially helpful for financial applications and other uses which require exact decimal representation, control over precision, control over rounding to meet legal or regulatory requirements, tracking of significant decimal places, or for applications where the user expects the results to match calculations done by hand.

For example, calculating a 5% tax on a 70 cent phone charge gives different results in decimal floating point and binary floating point. The difference becomes significant if the results are rounded to the nearest cent:

```
>>> from decimal import *
>>> Decimal('0.70') * Decimal('1.05')
Decimal("0.7350")
>>> .70 * 1.05
0.73499999999999999
```

The Decimal result keeps a trailing zero, automatically inferring four place significance from multiplicands with two place significance. Decimal reproduces mathematics as done by hand and avoids issues that can arise when binary floating point cannot exactly represent decimal quantities.

Exact representation enables the Decimal class to perform modulo calculations and equality tests that are unsuitable for binary floating point:

```
>>> Decimal('1.00') % Decimal('.10')
Decimal("0.00")
>>> 1.00 % 0.10
0.09999999999999995

>>> sum([Decimal('0.1')]*10) == Decimal('1.0')
True
>>> sum([0.1]*10) == 1.0
False
```

The decimal module provides arithmetic with as much precision as needed:

```
>>> getcontext().prec = 36
>>> Decimal(1) / Decimal(7)
Decimal("0.142857142857142857142857142857142857")
```

12   What Now?

Reading this tutorial has probably reinforced your interest in using Python—you should be eager to apply Python to solving your real-world problems. Where should you go to learn more?

This tutorial is part of Python's documentation set. Some other documents in the set are:

- *Python Library Reference Manual*:

  You should browse through this manual, which gives complete (though terse) reference material about types, functions, and the modules in the standard library. The standard Python distribution includes a *lot* of additional code. There are modules to read UNIX mailboxes, retrieve documents via HTTP, generate random numbers, parse command-line options, write CGI programs, compress data, and many other tasks. Skimming through the *Python Library Reference Manual* will give you an idea of what's available.

- *Installing Python Modules* explains how to install external modules written by other Python users.

- *Python Language Reference Manual*: A detailed explanation of Python's syntax and semantics. It's heavy reading, but is useful as a complete guide to the language itself.

More Python resources:

- http://www.python.org: The major Python Web site. It contains code, documentation, and pointers to Python-related pages around the Web. This Web site is mirrored in various places around the world, such as Europe, Japan, and Australia; a mirror may be faster than the main site, depending on your geographical location.

- http://docs.python.org: Fast access to Python's documentation.

- http://cheeseshop.python.org: The Python Package Index, nicknamed the Cheese Shop, is an index of user-created Python modules that are available for download. Once you begin releasing code, you can register it here so that others can find it.

- `http://aspn.activestate.com/ASPN/Python/Cookbook/`: The Python Cookbook is a sizable collection of code examples, larger modules, and useful scripts. Particularly notable contributions are collected in a book also titled *Python Cookbook* (O'Reilly & Associates, ISBN 0-596-00797-3.)

For Python-related questions and problem reports, you can post to the newsgroup `comp.lang.python`, or send them to the mailing list at `python-list@python.org`. The newsgroup and mailing list are gatewayed, so messages posted to one will automatically be forwarded to the other. There are around 120 postings a day (with peaks up to several hundred), asking (and answering) questions, suggesting new features, and announcing new modules.

Before posting, be sure to check the list of Frequently Asked Questions (also called the FAQ), or look for it in the 'Misc/' directory of the Python source distribution. Mailing list archives are available at `http://mail.python.org/`. The FAQ answers many of the questions that come up again and again, and may already contain the solution for your problem.

A Interactive Input Editing and History Substitution

Some versions of the Python interpreter support editing of the current input line and history substitution, similar to facilities found in the Korn shell and the GNU Bash shell. This is implemented using the *GNU Readline* library, which supports Emacs-style and vi-style editing. This library has its own documentation which I won't duplicate here; however, the basics are easily explained. The interactive editing and history described here are optionally available in the UNIX and Cygwin versions of the interpreter.

This chapter does *not* document the editing facilities of Mark Hammond's PythonWin package or the Tk-based environment, IDLE, distributed with Python. The command line history recall which operates within DOS boxes on NT and some other DOS and Windows flavors is yet another beast.

A.1 Line Editing

If supported, input line editing is active whenever the interpreter prints a primary or secondary prompt. The current line can be edited using the conventional Emacs control characters. The most important of these are: C-A (Control-A) moves the cursor to the beginning of the line, C-E to the end, C-B moves it one position to the left, C-F to the right. Backspace erases the character to the left of the cursor, C-D the character to its right. C-K kills (erases) the rest of the line to the right of the cursor, C-Y yanks back the last killed string. C-underscore undoes the last change you made; it can be repeated for cumulative effect.

A.2 History Substitution

History substitution works as follows. All non-empty input lines issued are saved in a history buffer, and when a new prompt is given you are positioned on a new line at the bottom of this buffer. C-P moves one line up (back) in the history buffer, C-N moves one down. Any line in the history buffer can be edited; an asterisk appears in front of the prompt to mark a line as modified. Pressing the Return key passes the current line to the interpreter. C-R starts an incremental reverse search; C-S starts a forward search.

A.3   Key Bindings

The key bindings and some other parameters of the Readline library can be customized by placing commands in an initialization file called '~/.inputrc'. Key bindings have the form

```
key-name: function-name
```

or

```
"string": function-name
```

and options can be set with

```
set option-name value
```

For example:

```
# I prefer vi-style editing:
set editing-mode vi

# Edit using a single line:
set horizontal-scroll-mode On

# Rebind some keys:
Meta-h: backward-kill-word
"\C-u": universal-argument
"\C-x\C-r": re-read-init-file
```

Note that the default binding for Tab in Python is to insert a Tab character instead of Readline's default filename completion function. If you insist, you can override this by putting

```
Tab: complete
```

in your '~/.inputrc'. (Of course, this makes it harder to type indented continuation lines if you're accustomed to using Tab for that purpose.)

Automatic completion of variable and module names is optionally available. To enable it in the interpreter's interactive mode, add the following to your startup file:[1]

```
import rlcompleter, readline
readline.parse_and_bind('tab: complete')
```

This binds the Tab key to the completion function, so hitting the Tab key twice suggests completions; it looks at Python statement names, the current local variables, and the available module names. For dotted expressions such as string.a, it will evaluate the expression up to the final '.' and then suggest completions from the attributes of the resulting object. Note that this may execute application-defined code if an object with a __getattr__() method is part of the expression.

A more capable startup file might look like this example. Note that this deletes the names it creates once they are no longer needed; this is done since the startup file is executed in the same namespace as the interactive commands, and removing the names avoids creating side effects in the interactive environment. You may find it convenient to keep some of the imported modules, such as os, which turn out to be needed in most sessions with the interpreter.

```
# Add auto-completion and a stored history file of
# commands to your Python interactive interpreter.
# Requires Python 2.0+, readline. Autocomplete is bound
# to the Esc key by default (you can change it - see
# readline docs).
#
# Store the file in ~/.pystartup, and set an
# environment variable to point to it: "export
# PYTHONSTARTUP=/home/guido/.pystartup" in bash.
#
# Note that PYTHONSTARTUP does *not* expand "~", so you
# have to put in the full path to your home directory.

import atexit
import os
import readline
import rlcompleter

historyPath = os.path.expanduser("~/.pyhistory")
```

---

[1]Python will execute the contents of a file identified by the PYTHONSTARTUP environment variable when you start an interactive interpreter.

```
def save_history(historyPath=historyPath):
    import readline
    readline.write_history_file(historyPath)

if os.path.exists(historyPath):
    readline.read_history_file(historyPath)

atexit.register(save_history)
del os, atexit, readline, rlcompleter
del save_history, historyPath
```

A.4   Commentary

This facility is an enormous step forward compared to earlier versions
of the interpreter; however, some wishes are left: It would be nice if the
proper indentation were suggested on continuation lines (the parser knows
if an indent token is required next). The completion mechanism might
use the interpreter's symbol table. A command to check (or even suggest)
matching parentheses, quotes, etc., would also be useful.

B Floating Point Arithmetic: Issues and Limitations

Floating-point numbers are represented in computer hardware as base 2 (binary) fractions. For example, the decimal fraction

    0.125

has value $1/10 + 2/100 + 5/1000$, and in the same way the binary fraction

    0.001

has value $0/2 + 0/4 + 1/8$. These two fractions have identical values, the only real difference being that the first is written in base 10 fractional notation, and the second in base 2.

Unfortunately, most decimal fractions cannot be represented exactly as binary fractions. A consequence is that, in general, the decimal floating-point numbers you enter are only approximated by the binary floating-point numbers actually stored in the machine.

The problem is easier to understand at first in base 10. Consider the fraction $1/3$. You can approximate that as a base 10 fraction:

    0.3

or, better,

    0.33

or, better,

    0.333

and so on. No matter how many digits you're willing to write down, the result will never be exactly $1/3$, but will be an increasingly better approximation of $1/3$.

In the same way, no matter how many base 2 digits you're willing to use, the decimal value 0.1 cannot be represented exactly as a base 2 fraction. In base 2, $1/10$ is the infinitely repeating fraction

0.000110011001100110011001100110011001100110011001100110011...

Stop at any finite number of bits, and you get an approximation. This is why you see things like:

```
>>> 0.1
0.10000000000000001
```

On most machines today, that is what you'll see if you enter 0.1 at a Python prompt. You may not, though, because the number of bits used by the hardware to store floating-point values can vary across machines, and Python only prints a decimal approximation to the true decimal value of the binary approximation stored by the machine. On most machines, if Python were to print the true decimal value of the binary approximation stored for 0.1, it would have to display

```
>>> 0.1
0.1000000000000000055511151231257827021181583404541015625
```

instead! The Python prompt uses the builtin repr() function to obtain a string version of everything it displays. For floats, repr(*float*) rounds the true decimal value to 17 significant digits, giving

```
0.10000000000000001
```

repr(*float*) produces 17 significant digits because it turns out that's enough (on most machines) so that eval(repr(x)) == x exactly for all finite floats x, but rounding to 16 digits is not enough to make that true.

Note that this is in the very nature of binary floating-point: this is not a bug in Python, and it is not a bug in your code either. You'll see the same kind of thing in all languages that support your hardware's floating-point arithmetic (although some languages may not *display* the difference by default, or in all output modes).

Python's builtin str() function produces only 12 significant digits, and you may wish to use that instead. It's unusual for eval(str(x)) to reproduce x, but the output may be more pleasant to look at:

```
>>> print str(0.1)
0.1
```

It's important to realize that this is, in a real sense, an illusion: the value in the machine is not exactly 1/10, you're simply rounding the *display* of the true machine value.

Other surprises follow from this one. For example, after seeing

```
>>> 0.1
0.10000000000000001
```

you may be tempted to use the round() function to chop it back to the single digit you expect. But that makes no difference:

```
>>> round(0.1, 1)
0.10000000000000001
```

The problem is that the binary floating-point value stored for "0.1" was already the best possible binary approximation to 1/10, so trying to round it again can't make it better: it was already as good as it gets.

Another consequence is that since 0.1 is not exactly 1/10, summing ten values of 0.1 may not yield exactly 1.0, either:

```
>>> sum = 0.0
>>> for i in range(10):
...     sum += 0.1
...
>>> sum
0.99999999999999989
```

Binary floating-point arithmetic holds many surprises like this. The problem with "0.1" is explained in precise detail below, in the "Representation Error" section. See *The Perils of Floating Point* at http://www.lahey.com/float.htm for a more complete account of other common surprises.

As that says near the end, "there are no easy answers." Still, don't be unduly wary of floating-point! The errors in Python float operations are inherited from the floating-point hardware, and on most machines are on the order of no more than 1 part in 2^{53} per operation. That's more than adequate for most tasks, but you do need to keep in mind that it's not decimal arithmetic, and that every float operation can suffer a new rounding error.

While pathological cases do exist, for most casual use of floating-point arithmetic you'll see the result you expect in the end if you simply round the display of your final results to the number of decimal digits you expect. str() usually suffices, and for finer control see the discussion of Python's % format operator: the %g, %f and %e format codes supply flexible and easy ways to round float results for display.

B.1 Representation Error

This section explains the "0.1" example in detail, and shows how you can perform an exact analysis of cases like this yourself. Basic familiarity with binary floating-point representation is assumed.

Representation error refers to the fact that most decimal fractions cannot be represented exactly as binary (base 2) fractions. This is the chief reason why Python (or Perl, C, C++, Java, Fortran, and many others) often won't display the exact decimal number you expect:

```
>>> 0.1
0.10000000000000001
```

Why is that? 1/10 is not exactly representable as a binary fraction. Almost all machines today use IEEE-754 floating point arithmetic, and almost all platforms map Python floats to IEEE-754 "double precision". IEEE-754 double precision numbers contain 53 bits of precision, so on input the computer strives to convert 0.1 to the closest fraction it can of the form $J/2^N$ where J is an integer containing exactly 53 bits. Rewriting

$$1/10 \approx J/2^N$$

as

$$J \approx 2^N/10$$

and recalling that J has exactly 53 bits (i.e. $2^{52} \leq J < 2^{53}$), the best value for N is 56:

```
>>> 2**52, 2**53
(4503599627370496, 9007199254740992)
>>> 2**56/10
7205759403792793
>>> 2**52 <= 2**56/10 < 2**53
True
```

That is, 56 is the only value for N that leaves J with exactly 53 bits. The best possible value for J is then that quotient rounded:

```
>>> q, r = divmod(2**56, 10)
>>> r
6L
```

Since the remainder is more than half of 10, the best approximation is obtained by rounding up:

```
>>> q+1
7205759403792794L
```

Therefore the best possible approximation to $1/10$ in double precision is that over 2^{56}, or

$$7205759403792794 \; / \; 72057594037927936$$

Note that since we rounded up, this is actually a little bit larger than $1/10$; if we had not rounded up, the quotient would have been a little bit smaller than $1/10$. But in no case can it be *exactly* $1/10$!

So the computer never "sees" $1/10$: what it sees is the exact fraction given above, the best double approximation it can get:

```
>>> .1 * 2**56
7205759403792794.0
```

If we multiply that fraction by 10^{30}, we can see the (truncated) value of its 30 most significant decimal digits:

```
>>> 7205759403792794 * 10**30 / 2**56
100000000000000005551115123125L
```

meaning that the exact number stored in the computer is approximately equal to the decimal value 0.100000000000000005551115123125. Rounding that to 17 significant digits gives the 0.10000000000000001 that Python displays (well, will display on any IEEE conforming platform that does best-possible input and output conversions in its C library—yours may not!).

C History and License

C.1 History of the software

Python was created in the early 1990s by Guido van Rossum at Stichting Mathematisch Centrum (CWI, see http://www.cwi.nl/) in the Netherlands as a successor of a language called ABC. Guido remains Python's principal author, although it includes many contributions from others.

In 1995, Guido continued his work on Python at the Corporation for National Research Initiatives (CNRI, see http://www.cnri.reston.va.us/) in Reston, Virginia where he released several versions of the software.

In May 2000, Guido and the Python core development team moved to BeOpen.com to form the BeOpen PythonLabs team. In October of the same year, the PythonLabs team moved to Digital Creations (now Zope Corporation; see http://www.zope.com/). In 2001, the Python Software Foundation (PSF, see http://www.python.org/psf/) was formed, a non-profit organization created specifically to own Python-related Intellectual Property. Zope Corporation is a sponsoring member of the PSF.

The license agreement for the current version of Python is given in the next section, along with the licenses used by previous versions. The table below summarizes the release history:

Release	Derived from	Year	Owner	GPL compatible?
0.9.0 thru 1.2	n/a	1991-1995	CWI	yes
1.3 thru 1.5.2	1.2	1995-1999	CNRI	yes
1.6	1.5.2	2000	CNRI	no
2.0	1.6	2000	BeOpen.com	no
1.6.1	1.6	2001	CNRI	no
2.1	2.0+1.6.1	2001	PSF	no
2.0.1	2.0+1.6.1	2001	PSF	yes
2.1.1	2.1+2.0.1	2001	PSF	yes
2.2	2.1.1	2001	PSF	yes
2.1.2	2.1.1	2002	PSF	yes
2.1.3	2.1.2	2002	PSF	yes
2.2.1	2.2	2002	PSF	yes
2.2.2	2.2.1	2002	PSF	yes
2.2.3	2.2.2	2002-2003	PSF	yes
2.3	2.2.2	2002-2003	PSF	yes
2.3.1	2.3	2002-2003	PSF	yes
2.3.2	2.3.1	2003	PSF	yes
2.3.3	2.3.2	2003	PSF	yes
2.3.4	2.3.3	2004	PSF	yes

2.3.5	2.3.4	2005	PSF	yes
2.4	2.3	2004	PSF	yes
2.4.1	2.4	2005	PSF	yes
2.4.2	2.4.1	2005	PSF	yes
2.4.3	2.4.2	2006	PSF	yes
2.5	2.4	2006	PSF	yes

Note: GPL-compatible means that it is possible to combine Python with other software that is released under the GNU General Public License. Thanks to the many outside volunteers who have worked under Guido's direction to make these releases possible.

C.2 Terms and conditions for Python

PSF LICENSE AGREEMENT FOR PYTHON 2.5

1. This LICENSE AGREEMENT is between the Python Software Foundation ("PSF"), and the Individual or Organization ("Licensee") accessing and otherwise using Python 2.5 software in source or binary form and its associated documentation.

2. Subject to the terms and conditions of this License Agreement, PSF hereby grants Licensee a nonexclusive, royalty-free, world-wide license to reproduce, analyze, test, perform and/or display publicly, prepare derivative works, distribute, and otherwise use Python 2.5 alone or in any derivative version, provided, however, that PSF's License Agreement and PSF's notice of copyright, i.e., "Copyright © 2001-2006 Python Software Foundation; All Rights Reserved" are retained in Python 2.5 alone or in any derivative version prepared by Licensee.

3. In the event Licensee prepares a derivative work that is based on or incorporates Python 2.5 or any part thereof, and wants to make the derivative work available to others as provided herein, then Licensee hereby agrees to include in any such work a brief summary of the changes made to Python 2.5.

4. PSF is making Python 2.5 available to Licensee on an "AS IS" basis. PSF MAKES NO REPRESENTATIONS OR WARRANTIES, EXPRESS OR IMPLIED. BY WAY OF EXAMPLE, BUT NOT LIMITATION, PSF MAKES NO AND DISCLAIMS ANY REPRESENTATION OR WARRANTY OF MERCHANTABILITY OR FITNESS FOR ANY PARTICULAR PURPOSE OR THAT THE USE OF PYTHON 2.5 WILL NOT INFRINGE ANY THIRD PARTY RIGHTS.

5. PSF SHALL NOT BE LIABLE TO LICENSEE OR ANY OTHER USERS OF PYTHON 2.5 FOR ANY INCIDENTAL, SPECIAL, OR CONSEQUENTIAL DAMAGES OR LOSS AS A RESULT OF MODIFYING, DISTRIBUTING, OR OTHERWISE USING PYTHON 2.5, OR ANY DERIVATIVE THEREOF, EVEN IF ADVISED OF THE POSSIBILITY THEREOF.

6. This License Agreement will automatically terminate upon a material breach of its terms and conditions.

7. Nothing in this License Agreement shall be deemed to create any relationship of agency, partnership, or joint venture between PSF and Licensee. This License Agreement does not grant permission to use PSF trademarks or trade name in a trademark sense to endorse or promote products or services of Licensee, or any third party.

8. By copying, installing or otherwise using Python 2.5, Licensee agrees to be bound by the terms and conditions of this License Agreement.

BEOPEN.COM LICENSE AGREEMENT FOR PYTHON 2.0
BEOPEN PYTHON OPEN SOURCE LICENSE AGREEMENT VERSION 1

1. This LICENSE AGREEMENT is between BeOpen.com ("BeOpen"), having an office at 160 Saratoga Avenue, Santa Clara, CA 95051, and the Individual or Organization ("Licensee") accessing and otherwise using this software in source or binary form and its associated documentation ("the Software").

2. Subject to the terms and conditions of this BeOpen Python License Agreement, BeOpen hereby grants Licensee a non-exclusive, royalty-free, world-wide license to reproduce, analyze, test, perform and/or display publicly, prepare derivative works, distribute, and otherwise use the Software alone or in any derivative version, provided, however, that the BeOpen Python License is retained in the Software, alone or in any derivative version prepared by Licensee.

3. BeOpen is making the Software available to Licensee on an "AS IS" basis. BEOPEN MAKES NO REPRESENTATIONS OR WARRANTIES, EXPRESS OR IMPLIED. BY WAY OF EXAMPLE, BUT NOT LIMITATION, BEOPEN MAKES NO AND DISCLAIMS ANY REPRESENTATION OR WARRANTY OF MERCHANTABILITY OR FITNESS FOR ANY PARTICULAR PURPOSE OR THAT THE USE OF THE SOFTWARE WILL NOT INFRINGE ANY THIRD PARTY RIGHTS.

4. BEOPEN SHALL NOT BE LIABLE TO LICENSEE OR ANY OTHER USERS OF THE SOFTWARE FOR ANY INCIDENTAL, SPECIAL, OR CONSEQUENTIAL DAMAGES OR LOSS AS A RESULT OF USING, MODIFYING OR DISTRIBUTING THE SOFTWARE, OR ANY DERIVATIVE THEREOF, EVEN IF ADVISED OF THE POSSIBILITY THEREOF.

5. This License Agreement will automatically terminate upon a material breach of its terms and conditions.

6. This License Agreement shall be governed by and interpreted in all respects by the law of the State of California, excluding conflict of law provisions. Nothing in this License Agreement shall be deemed to create any relationship of agency, partnership, or joint venture between BeOpen and Licensee. This License Agreement does not grant permission to use BeOpen trademarks or trade names in a trademark sense to endorse or promote products or services of Licensee, or any third party. As an exception, the "BeOpen Python" logos available at http://www.pythonlabs.com/logos.html may be used according to the permissions granted on that web page.

7. By copying, installing or otherwise using the software, Licensee agrees to be bound by the terms and conditions of this License Agreement.

CNRI LICENSE AGREEMENT FOR PYTHON 1.6.1

1. This LICENSE AGREEMENT is between the Corporation for National Research Initiatives, having an office at 1895 Preston White Drive, Reston, VA 20191 ("CNRI"), and the Individual or Organization ("Licensee") accessing and otherwise using Python 1.6.1 software in source or binary form and its associated documentation.

2. Subject to the terms and conditions of this License Agreement, CNRI hereby grants Licensee a nonexclusive, royalty-free, world-wide license to reproduce,

analyze, test, perform and/or display publicly, prepare derivative works, distribute, and otherwise use Python 1.6.1 alone or in any derivative version, provided, however, that CNRI's License Agreement and CNRI's notice of copyright, i.e., "Copyright © 1995-2001 Corporation for National Research Initiatives; All Rights Reserved" are retained in Python 1.6.1 alone or in any derivative version prepared by Licensee. Alternately, in lieu of CNRI's License Agreement, Licensee may substitute the following text (omitting the quotes): "Python 1.6.1 is made available subject to the terms and conditions in CNRI's License Agreement. This Agreement together with Python 1.6.1 may be located on the Internet using the following unique, persistent identifier (known as a handle): 1895.22/1013. This Agreement may also be obtained from a proxy server on the Internet using the following URL: http://hdl.handle.net/1895.22/1013."

3. In the event Licensee prepares a derivative work that is based on or incorporates Python 1.6.1 or any part thereof, and wants to make the derivative work available to others as provided herein, then Licensee hereby agrees to include in any such work a brief summary of the changes made to Python 1.6.1.

4. CNRI is making Python 1.6.1 available to Licensee on an "AS IS" basis. CNRI MAKES NO REPRESENTATIONS OR WARRANTIES, EXPRESS OR IMPLIED. BY WAY OF EXAMPLE, BUT NOT LIMITATION, CNRI MAKES NO AND DISCLAIMS ANY REPRESENTATION OR WARRANTY OF MERCHANTABILITY OR FITNESS FOR ANY PARTICULAR PURPOSE OR THAT THE USE OF PYTHON 1.6.1 WILL NOT INFRINGE ANY THIRD PARTY RIGHTS.

5. CNRI SHALL NOT BE LIABLE TO LICENSEE OR ANY OTHER USERS OF PYTHON 1.6.1 FOR ANY INCIDENTAL, SPECIAL, OR CONSEQUENTIAL DAMAGES OR LOSS AS A RESULT OF MODIFYING, DISTRIBUTING, OR OTHERWISE USING PYTHON 1.6.1, OR ANY DERIVATIVE THEREOF, EVEN IF ADVISED OF THE POSSIBILITY THEREOF.

6. This License Agreement will automatically terminate upon a material breach of its terms and conditions.

7. This License Agreement shall be governed by the federal intellectual property law of the United States, including without limitation the federal copyright law, and, to the extent such U.S. federal law does not apply, by the law of the Commonwealth of Virginia, excluding Virginia's conflict of law provisions. Notwithstanding the foregoing, with regard to derivative works based on Python 1.6.1 that incorporate non-separable material that was previously distributed under the GNU General Public License (GPL), the law of the Commonwealth of Virginia shall govern this License Agreement only as to issues arising under or with respect to Paragraphs 4, 5, and 7 of this License Agreement. Nothing in this License Agreement shall be deemed to create any relationship of agency, partnership, or joint venture between CNRI and Licensee. This License Agreement does not grant permission to use CNRI trademarks or trade name in a trademark sense to endorse or promote products or services of Licensee, or any third party.

8. By clicking on the "ACCEPT" button where indicated, or by copying, installing or otherwise using Python 1.6.1, Licensee agrees to be bound by the terms and conditions of this License Agreement.

ACCEPT

CWI LICENSE AGREEMENT FOR PYTHON 0.9.0 THROUGH 1.2

Copyright © 1991 1995, Stichting Mathematisch Centrum Amsterdam, The Netherlands. All rights reserved.

C.3 Other licenses and acknowledgements

This section is an incomplete, but growing list of licenses and acknowledgements for third-party software incorporated in the Python distribution.

C.3.1 Mersenne Twister

Any feedback is very welcome. http://www.math.keio.ac.jp/matumoto/emt.html email: matumoto@math.keio.ac.jp

C.3.2 Sockets

The socket module uses the functions, getaddrinfo, and getnameinfo, which are coded in separate source files from the WIDE Project[1].

Copyright (C) 1995, 1996, 1997, and 1998 WIDE Project. All rights reserved.

C.3.3 Floating point exception control

The source for the fpectl module includes the following notice:

C.3.4 MD5 message digest algorithm

The source code for the md5 module contains the following notice:

Copyright (C) 1999, 2002 Aladdin Enterprises. All rights reserved.

---

[1] http://www.wide.ad.jp/about/index.html

Independent implementation of MD5 (RFC 1321).

This code implements the MD5 Algorithm defined in RFC 1321, whose text is available at http://www.ietf.org/rfc/rfc1321.txt The code is derived from the text of the RFC, including the test suite (section A.5) but excluding the rest of Appendix A. It does not include any code or documentation that is identified in the RFC as being copyrighted.

The original and principal author of md5.h is L. Peter Deutsch <ghost@aladdin.com>. Other authors are noted in the change history that follows (in reverse chronological order):

2002-04-13 lpd Removed support for non-ANSI compilers; removed references to Ghostscript; clarified derivation from RFC 1321; now handles byte order either statically or dynamically. 1999-11-04 lpd Edited comments slightly for automatic TOC extraction. 1999-10-18 lpd Fixed typo in header comment (ansi2knr rather than md5); added conditionalization for C++ compilation from Martin Purschke <purschke@bnl.gov>. 1999-05-03 lpd Original version.

C.3.5   Asynchronous socket services

The asynchat and asyncore modules contain the following notice:

C.3.6   Cookie management

The Cookie module contains the following notice:

Timothy O'Malley DISCLAIMS ALL WARRANTIES WITH REGARD TO THIS SOFT-
WARE, INCLUDING ALL IMPLIED WARRANTIES OF MERCHANTABILITY AND
FITNESS, IN NO EVENT SHALL Timothy O'Malley BE LIABLE FOR ANY SPECIAL,
INDIRECT OR CONSEQUENTIAL DAMAGES OR ANY DAMAGES WHATSOEVER
RESULTING FROM LOSS OF USE, DATA OR PROFITS, WHETHER IN AN ACTION
OF CONTRACT, NEGLIGENCE OR OTHER TORTIOUS ACTION, ARISING OUT OF
OR IN CONNECTION WITH THE USE OR PERFORMANCE OF THIS SOFTWARE.

C.3.7 Profiling

The profile and pstats modules contain the following notice:

Copyright 1994, by InfoSeek Corporation, all rights reserved. Written by James Roskind

Permission to use, copy, modify, and distribute this Python software and its associated documentation for any purpose (subject to the restriction in the following sentence) without fee
is hereby granted, provided that the above copyright notice appears in all copies, and that
both that copyright notice and this permission notice appear in supporting documentation,
and that the name of InfoSeek not be used in advertising or publicity pertaining to distribution of the software without specific, written prior permission. This permission is explicitly
restricted to the copying and modification of the software to remain in Python, compiled
Python, or other languages (such as C) wherein the modified or derived code is exclusively
imported into a Python module.

INFOSEEK CORPORATION DISCLAIMS ALL WARRANTIES WITH REGARD TO
THIS SOFTWARE, INCLUDING ALL IMPLIED WARRANTIES OF MERCHANTABIL-
ITY AND FITNESS. IN NO EVENT SHALL INFOSEEK CORPORATION BE LI-
ABLE FOR ANY SPECIAL, INDIRECT OR CONSEQUENTIAL DAMAGES OR ANY
DAMAGES WHATSOEVER RESULTING FROM LOSS OF USE, DATA OR PROFITS,
WHETHER IN AN ACTION OF CONTRACT, NEGLIGENCE OR OTHER TORTIOUS
ACTION, ARISING OUT OF OR IN CONNECTION WITH THE USE OR PERFOR-
MANCE OF THIS SOFTWARE.

C.3.8 Execution tracing

The trace module contains the following notice:

portions copyright 2001, Autonomous Zones Industries, Inc., all rights... err... reserved
and offered to the public under the terms of the Python 2.2 license. Author: Zooko
O'Whielacronx http://zooko.com/ mailto:zooko@zooko.com

Copyright 2000, Mojam Media, Inc., all rights reserved. Author: Skip Montanaro

Copyright 1999, Bioreason, Inc., all rights reserved. Author: Andrew Dalke

Copyright 1995-1997, Automatrix, Inc., all rights reserved. Author: Skip Montanaro

Copyright 1991-1995, Stichting Mathematisch Centrum, all rights reserved.

Permission to use, copy, modify, and distribute this Python software and its associated documentation for any purpose without fee is hereby granted, provided that the above copyright
notice appears in all copies, and that both that copyright notice and this permission
notice appear in supporting documentation, and that the name of neither Automatrix, Bioreason
or Mojam Media be used in advertising or publicity pertaining to distribution of the software
without specific, written prior permission.

C.3.9 UUencode and UUdecode functions

The uu module contains the following notice:

Copyright 1994 by Lance Ellinghouse Cathedral City, California Republic, United States of
America. All Rights Reserved Permission to use, copy, modify, and distribute this software
and its documentation for any purpose and without fee is hereby granted, provided that the

Modified by Jack Jansen, CWI, July 1995: Use binascii module to do the actual line-by-line conversion between ascii and binary. This results in a 1000-fold speedup. The C version is still 5 times faster, though. Arguments more compliant with python standard

C.3.10   XML Remote Procedure Calls

The xmlrpclib module contains the following notice:

The XML-RPC client interface is

D Glossary

>>> The typical Python prompt of the interactive shell. Often seen for code examples that can be tried right away in the interpreter.

... The typical Python prompt of the interactive shell when entering code for an indented code block.

BDFL Benevolent Dictator For Life, a.k.a. Guido van Rossum, Python's creator.

byte code The internal representation of a Python program in the interpreter. The byte code is also cached in .pyc and .pyo files so that executing the same file is faster the second time (recompilation from source to byte code can be avoided). This "intermediate language" is said to run on a "virtual machine" that calls the subroutines corresponding to each bytecode.

classic class Any class which does not inherit from object. See *new-style class*.

coercion The implicit conversion of an instance of one type to another during an operation which involves two arguments of the same type. For example, int(3.15) converts the floating point number to the integer 3, but in 3+4.5, each argument is of a different type (one int, one float), and both must be converted to the same type before they can be added or it will raise a TypeError. Coercion between two operands can be performed with the coerce builtin function; thus, 3+4.5 is equivalent to calling operator.add(*coerce(3, 4. 5)) and results in operator.add(3.0, 4.5).[1] Without coercion, all arguments of even compatible types would have to be normalized to the same value by the programmer, e.g., float(3)+4.5 rather than just 3+4.5.

complex number An extension of the familiar real number system in which all numbers are expressed as a sum of a real part and an imaginary part. Imaginary numbers are real multiples of the imaginary unit (the square root of -1), often written i in mathematics or j in engineering. Python has builtin support for complex numbers,

---

[1]This requires the operator module. Type import operator; help(operator); for details.

which are written with this latter notation; the imaginary part is written with a j suffix, e.g., 3+1j. To get access to complex equivalents of the math module, use cmath. Use of complex numbers is a fairly advanced mathematical feature. If you're not aware of a need for them, it's almost certain you can safely ignore them.

descriptor Any *new-style* object that defines the methods __get__(), __set__(), or __delete__(). When a class attribute is a descriptor, its special binding behavior is triggered upon attribute lookup. Normally, writing *a.b* looks up the object *b* in the class dictionary for *a*, but if *b* is a descriptor, the defined method gets called. Understanding descriptors is a key to a deep understanding of Python because they are the basis for many features including functions, methods, properties, class methods, static methods, and reference to super classes.

dictionary An associative array, where arbitrary keys are mapped to values. The use of dict much resembles that for list, but the keys can be any object with a __hash__() function, not just integers starting from zero. Called a hash in Perl.

duck-typing Pythonic programming style that determines an object's type by inspection of its method or attribute signature rather than by explicit relationship to some type object ("If it looks like a duck and quacks like a duck, it must be a duck.") By emphasizing interfaces rather than specific types, well-designed code improves its flexibility by allowing polymorphic substitution. Duck-typing avoids tests using type() or isinstance(). Instead, it typically employs hasattr() tests or *EAFP* programming.

EAFP Easier to ask for forgiveness than permission. This common Python coding style assumes the existence of valid keys or attributes and catches exceptions if the assumption proves false. This clean and fast style is characterized by the presence of many try and except statements. The technique contrasts with the *LBYL* style that is common in many other languages such as C.

__future__ A pseudo module which programmers can use to enable new language features which are not compatible with the current interpreter. For example, the expression 11/4 currently evaluates to 2. If the module in which it is executed had enabled *true division* by executing:

```
from __future__ import division
```

the expression 11/4 would evaluate to 2.75. By importing the __future__ module and evaluating its variables, you can see when a new feature was first added to the language and when it will become the default:

```
>>> import __future__
>>> __future__.division
_Feature((2, 2, 0, 'alpha', 2), (3, 0, 0, 'alpha', 0),
    8192)
```

generator A function that returns an iterator. It looks like a normal function except that values are returned to the caller using a yield statement instead of a return statement. Generator functions often contain one or more for or while loops that yield elements back to the caller. The function execution is stopped at the yield keyword (returning the result) and is resumed there when the next element is requested by calling the next() method of the returned iterator.

generator expression An expression that returns a generator. It looks like a normal expression followed by a for expression defining a loop variable, range, and an optional if expression. The combined expression generates values for an enclosing function:

```
>>> sum(i*i for i in range(10))   # sum of squares
                                  # 0, 1, 4, ... 81
285
```

GIL See *global interpreter lock.*

global interpreter lock The lock used by Python threads to assure that only one thread can be run at a time. This simplifies Python by assuring that no two processes can access the same memory at the same time. Locking the entire interpreter makes it easier for the interpreter to be multi-threaded, at the expense of some parallelism on multi-processor machines. Efforts have been made in the past to create a "free-threaded" interpreter (one which locks shared data at a much finer granularity), but performance suffered in the common single-processor case.

IDLE An Integrated Development Environment for Python. IDLE is a basic editor and interpreter environment that ships with the standard distribution of Python. Good for beginners, it also serves as clear example code for those wanting to implement a moderately sophisticated, multi-platform GUI application.

immutable An object with fixed value. Immutable objects are numbers, strings or tuples (and more). Such an object cannot be altered. A new object has to be created if a different value has to be stored. They play an important role in places where a constant hash value is needed, for example as a key in a dictionary.

integer division Mathematical division discarding any remainder. For example, the expression 11/4 currently evaluates to 2 in contrast to the 2.75 returned by float division. Also called *floor division*. When dividing two integers the outcome will always be another integer (having the floor function applied to it). However, if one of the operands is another numeric type (such as a float), the result will be coerced (see *coercion*) to a common type. For example, an integer divided by a float will result in a float value, possibly with a decimal fraction. Integer division can be forced by using the // operator instead of the / operator. See also __future__.

interactive Python has an interactive interpreter which means that you can try out things and immediately see their results. Just launch python with no arguments (possibly by selecting it from your computer's main menu). It is a very powerful way to test out new ideas or inspect modules and packages (remember help(x)).

interpreted Python is an interpreted language, as opposed to a compiled one. This means that the source files can be run directly without first creating an executable which is then run. Interpreted languages typically have a shorter development/debug cycle than compiled ones, though their programs generally also run more slowly. See also *interactive*.

iterable A container object capable of returning its members one at a time. Examples of iterables include all sequence types (such as list, str, and tuple) and some non-sequence types like dict and file and objects of any classes you define with an __iter__() or __getitem__() method. Iterables can be used in a for loop and in many other places where a sequence is needed (zip(), map(), ...). When an iterable object is passed as an argument to the builtin function iter(), it returns an iterator for the object. This iterator is good for one pass over the set of values. When using iterables, it is usually not necessary to call iter() or deal with iterator objects yourself. The for statement does that automatically for you, creating a temporary unnamed variable to hold the iterator for the duration of the loop. See also *iterator*, *sequence*, and *generator*.

iterator An object representing a stream of data. Repeated calls to the iterator's next() method return successive items in the stream.

When no more data is available a StopIteration exception is raised instead. At this point, the iterator object is exhausted and any further calls to its next() method just raise StopIteration again. Iterators are required to have an __iter__() method that returns the iterator object itself so every iterator is also iterable and may be used in most places where other iterables are accepted. One notable exception is code that attempts multiple iteration passes. A container object (such as a list) produces a fresh new iterator each time you pass it to the iter() function or use it in a for loop. Attempting this with an iterator will just return the same exhausted iterator object used in the previous iteration pass, making it appear like an empty container.

LBYL Look before you leap. This coding style explicitly tests for preconditions before making calls or lookups. This style contrasts with the *EAFP* approach and is characterized by the presence of many if statements.

list comprehension A compact way to process all or a subset of elements in a sequence and return a list with the results. result = ["0x%02x" %x for x in range(256) if x %2 == 0] generates a list of strings containing hex numbers (0x..) that are even and in the range from 0 to 255. The if clause is optional. If omitted, all elements in range(256) are processed.

mapping A container object (such as dict) that supports arbitrary key lookups using the special method __getitem__().

metaclass The class of a class. Class definitions create a class name, a class dictionary, and a list of base classes. The metaclass is responsible for taking those three arguments and creating the class. Most object oriented programming languages provide a default implementation. What makes Python special is that it is possible to create custom metaclasses. Most users never need this tool, but when the need arises, metaclasses can provide powerful, elegant solutions. They have been used for logging attribute access, adding thread-safety, tracking object creation, implementing singletons, and many other tasks.

mutable Mutable objects can change their value but keep their id(). See also *immutable*.

namespace The place where a variable is stored. Namespaces are implemented as dictionaries. There are the local, global and builtin namespaces as well as nested namespaces in objects (in methods). Namespaces support modularity by preventing naming conflicts. For instance, the functions `__builtin__.open()` and `os.open()` are distinguished by their namespaces. Namespaces also aid readability and maintainability by making it clear which module implements a function. For instance, writing `random.seed()` or `itertools.izip()` makes it clear that those functions are implemented by the `random` and `itertools` modules respectively.

nested scope The ability to refer to a variable in an enclosing definition. For instance, a function defined inside another function can refer to variables in the outer function. Note that nested scopes work only for reference and not for assignment which will always write to the innermost scope. In contrast, local variables both read and write in the innermost scope. Likewise, global variables read and write to the global namespace.

new-style class Any class that inherits from `object`. This includes all built-in types like `list` and `dict`. Only new-style classes can use Python's newer, versatile features like `__slots__`, descriptors, properties, `__getattribute__()`, class methods, and static methods.

Python3000 A mythical python release, not required to be backward compatible, with telepathic interface.

__slots__ A declaration inside a *new-style class* that saves memory by pre-declaring space for instance attributes and eliminating instance dictionaries. Though popular, the technique is somewhat tricky to get right and is best reserved for rare cases where there are large numbers of instances in a memory-critical application.

sequence An *iterable* which supports efficient element access using integer indices via the `__getitem__()` and `__len__()` special methods. Some built-in sequence types are `list`, `str`, `tuple`, and `unicode`. Note that `dict` also supports `__getitem__()` and `__len__()`, but is considered a mapping rather than a sequence because the lookups use arbitrary *immutable* keys rather than integers.

Zen of Python Listing of Python design principles and philosophies that are helpful in understanding and using the language. The listing can be found by typing "import this" at the interactive prompt.

E   Other books from the publisher

Network Theory publishes books about free software under free documentation licenses. Our current catalogue includes the following titles:

- **Python Language Reference Manual** by Guido van Rossum and Fred L. Drake, Jr. (ISBN 0-9541617-8-5) $19.95 (£12.95)

  This manual is the official reference for the Python language itself. It describes the syntax of Python and its built-in datatypes in depth, This manual is suitable for readers who need to be familiar with the details and rules of the Python language and its object system. For each copy of this manual sold, $1 is donated to the Python Software Foundation.

- **An Introduction to GCC** by Brian J. Gough, foreword by Richard M. Stallman. (ISBN 0-9541617-9-3) $19.95 (£12.95)

  This manual provides a tutorial introduction to the GNU C and C++ compilers, gcc and g++. Many books teach the C and C++ languages, but this book explains how to use the compiler itself. Based on years of observation of questions posted on mailing lists, it guides the reader straight to the important options of GCC.

  Concisely written, with numerous easy-to-follow "Hello World" examples, this book features a special foreword by Richard M. Stallman, principal developer of GCC and founder of the GNU Project.

- **GNU Bash Reference Manual** by Chet Ramey and Brian Fox (ISBN 0-9541617-7-7) $29.95 (£19.95)

  This manual is the definitive reference for GNU Bash, the standard GNU command-line interpreter. GNU Bash is a complete implementation of the POSIX.2 Bourne shell specification, with additional features from the C-shell and Korn shell. For each copy of this manual sold, $1 is donated to the Free Software Foundation.

- **Comparing and Merging Files with GNU diff and patch** by David MacKenzie, Paul Eggert, and Richard Stallman (ISBN 0-9541617-5-0) $19.95 (£12.95)

  This manual describes how to compare and merge files using GNU diff and patch. It includes an extensive tutorial that guides the reader through all the options of the diff and patch commands. Later chapters cover powerful time-saving techniques such as automatic merging of divergent branches of a source tree.

This is a printed copy of the official GNU diffutils manual. It documents all the diffutils programs (diff, cmp, sdiff, diff3), plus GNU patch. For each copy of this manual sold, $1 is donated to the Free Software Foundation.

- **Version Management with CVS** by Per Cederqvist et al. (ISBN 0-9541617-1-8) $29.95 (£19.95)

  This manual describes how to use CVS, the concurrent versioning system—one of the most widely-used source-code management systems available today. The manual provides tutorial examples for new users of CVS, as well as the definitive reference documentation for every CVS command and configuration option.

- **GNU Octave Manual** by John W. Eaton (ISBN 0-9541617-2-6) $29.99 (£19.99)

  This manual is the definitive guide to GNU Octave, an interactive environment for numerical computation with matrices and vectors. For each copy sold $1 is donated to the GNU Octave Development Fund.

- **An Introduction to R** by W.N. Venables, D.M. Smith and the R Development Core Team (ISBN 0-9541617-4-2) $19.95 (£12.95)

  This tutorial manual provides a comprehensive introduction to GNU R, a free software package for statistical computing and graphics.

- **The R Reference Manual—Base Package (Volumes 1 and 2)** by the R Development Core Team (ISBN 0-9546120-0-0) $69.95 each (£39.95 each)

  This manual is the first volume of the complete reference manual for the base package of GNU R, a free software environment for statistical computing and graphics. The main commands of the base package of R are described in the first volume, while other functions (such as graphics) are described in volume two.

  For each set of manuals sold (volumes 1 & 2), $10 is donated to the R Foundation.

All titles are available for order from bookstores worldwide.

Sales of the manuals fund the development of more free software and documentation.

For details, visit the website http://www.network-theory.co.uk/

Index

Symbols

N

O

P

Printed in the United States
127101LV00004B/65/A

9 780954 161767